John Dixon is a part-time writer living with his family in Bedfordshire. He decided to write modern poetry about observations of modern life before a sudden need for a heart valve replacement gave him a new subject to write about. Thankfully, he is still living with his family in Bedfordshire.

This book is dedicated to all the patients and staff from the assessment ward annex and the cardiac ward at Luton and Dunstable Hospital, and maple and cedar wards at Harefield Hospital, whom I had the pleasure to meet and share experiences with during March and April 2018. I wish all of you good times and a healthy rest of your lives; I hope I never see you again in the same circumstances!

Thank you to all the visitors who came in and made me laugh, shared a chat or a cry and a coffee and paid for the privilege. Thank you to Lucy and the family for cutting my nails, massaging my feet and bringing in secret chocolate and crisps.

"I was so full of antibiotics, I sneezed and the guy in the bed opposite got better." (Derek East, Bay D inmate, March 2018)

John Dixon

FOUR IN A BAY

A Pocket A to Z Guide
to Survival as a Patient
in the NHS

AUSTIN MACAULEY PUBLISHERS™
LONDON • CAMBRIDGE • NEW YORK • SHARJAH

A CIP catalogue record for this title is available from the British Library.

ISBN 9781528925686 (Paperback)
ISBN 9781528964395 (ePub e-book)

www.austinmacauley.com

First Published (2020)
Austin Macauley Publishers Ltd
25 Canada Square
Canary Wharf
London
E14 5LQ

Table of Contents

Introduction

Until recently, my dealings with the great British medical system had been, fortunately, sparse. I had never been an inpatient. I had sat in a 1970s laboratory at the age of seven placing wooden pegs into holes, while monotone sounds of different loudness went off in my ears and a doctor concluded, what wedding guests at my cousins wedding three weeks before had already concluded without any medical experience amongst them, that I was completely deaf in one ear. A simple question from a guest to my mum was that have you noticed he turns his head to whoever is speaking to him, I think he is deaf? My mum, never responsive to anything medical apart from fainting at the sight of blood, ignored it, as did I, because I didn't hear the question. However, after some home diagnosis (she shouted at me in each ear and then prodded each ear with the rounded end of a hair clip, her normal answer to most ear problems), she eventually gave in and off we went. The very flat line of response from one ear and the normal response from the other on the chart confirmed the doctor's diagnosis. To this day, 48 years later, my mum denies remembering that incident, denies that I was ever deaf and still uses hairpins on my dad when he says he can't hear anything.

I have visited people in hospital: my mum and dad a few times after various falling over incidents, they attribute to old age and I attribute to my mum being too nosey and careless; a school friend who had their appendix out when we were teenagers; and my wife twice when she had an operation on the NHS 35 years ago and an operation privately 10 years ago. The level of care in both instances was fantastic, the private operation experience difference was the private room, flat screen TV that worked and a view across the fields to tree-lined horizons. The NHS experience was a ward run by matron, who clearly was a student of old prison methods with a complete block on any incoming news, a window view of the wall holding up the old Victorian asylum block and lights out at seven (and on at six).

So, as I say, a limited view of hospital life. Of course, I had watched the Carry on Matron and Carry on Doctor series of films, a light-hearted view of hospital routines but based on the very real background of how regimentally hospitals were run in the 50s and 60s. There was an emphasis on discipline that many would like to see come back today and the absence of which many see as the reason for the failure of the NHS (my mum is one of those but then she is also in favour of bringing back capital punishment, the cane and the slipper at school and spam for lunch).

So, when I caught a cold, which then became a chest infection, I went to the doctors and asked for antibiotics which duly cleared up the infection. However, I seemed to be constantly breathless and that did not clear up; the doctor said I had an irregular heartbeat, I argued that it was me fighting infection but he wasn't convinced. My wife was not convinced either and one Sunday morning, she said that she was going to pack a small overnight bag and take me to A and E. Unable to fight off the breathlessness with the rounded end of a hairclip or by drinking a near fatal dose of milk of magnesia or by covering myself in Savlon (my mum's other cure all methods), I gave up looking for excuses and went in. Forever the optimist, I felt that some more antibiotics and a day of rest would cure all. Imagine my shock when, after scans and needles and X-rays and visits from a number of quizzical looking doctors, I was told the diagnosis was heart failure.

Heart failure! Being told that you have heart failure when you have never experienced any symptoms, apart from feeling a bit unfit, is like being given a whack in the nether regions, which at the time I would have preferred. However, unlike many of the people I was going to meet in the coming days and weeks, I (or my very observant wife, to be precise) had made the decision to come into hospital on my own and was not rushed to hospital in the back of an ambulance with a blue light. So, I had a head start on the game and for that, I was thoroughly grateful. I was mobile and independent, which takes off much of the strain from which many patients suffer. And so, began the journey I was not expecting, a journey that many people least expect to go on but have forced upon them. It is a journey into the Great British's medical institution, we call the NHS, often much maligned, run down and abused. How would I find this medical monster, now I was going to see it from the patient's perspective? A view from the inside was too good an opportunity to miss. I decided to document my experiences, so I have some memories of this unexpected interruption to my life and also to give those about to go through it, going through it or who have been through it, some optimism that a stay in the NHS is not as bad as the tabloids will sometimes tell us. I decided that in documenting it, I would offer my advice on what improved my life experience and also what left me depressed and dejected. As they always say in management training, planning and preparation is everything.

My Journey

Many middle-aged writers, comedians or presenters have a mid-life crisis and then go travelling—either with a sketchbook, a ukulele, a family member, a small tent or a dog or some other prop—writing about their travels in witty conversational books and hoping for a TV series. Michael Portillo and others travel around on trains with their Victorian travel books as companions. I had no intention of writing a mid-life crisis travel book, I had amused myself writing niche history books and moaning middle-aged man's poetry. Yet I was about to go on a completely unexpected journey myself, not as part of a mid-life crisis but as part of a very real-life crisis. The journey I took from the moment my wife deposited me on the doorstep of the NHS to the moment I arrived home again was an eight-week journey consisting of many quiet times interspersed with bursts of activity and culminating in an operation on my heart. It occurred to me from the early stages of my stay that here was the opportunity to write the ultimate travel book with no props or books and not actually boarding a train or setting up a tent or, in fact, going anywhere. All I had was a small bag of things, an Enterprise 5000 bed as transport and a destination somewhere in the unknown future. It would be difficult to record this episode as a story or diary, and so I have approached this task in the manner of a glossary, which picks out the highlights and lowlights of a stay in the NHS. These observations are an amalgamation of the four wards and two hospitals I stayed in before release. In my first abode, I spent a lot of time waiting to move hospitals and I was left relatively alone. The reader should also be aware, as I was very thankfully aware, that although I was ill, I was very mobile, able to walk around, shower and leave the ward. It gave me the opportunity to observe many aspects of a hospital in action and to talk to people and therefore, gave me an insight into hospital life, both from a patient and an employee view. I became friends with cleaners, visitors, housekeepers, nurses, doctors, tea ladies and patients. I watched patients come and go and I still believe some of the nurses and patients thought that I was a phoney, a secret shopper brought in to rate the NHS, prepared to put my body on the line through scans and medication, to report back on the real state of the NHS. I was asked to participate in student exam assessments, I was the subject of an internal audit and I was used as a test model for heart nurses on their training. I was even well enough looking to be asked to be in a photo with the nurses for publicity shots. My diagnosis was of interest to the doctors as it was considered a rare diagnosis. After four weeks on the cardiac ward, I started to question whether there was a secret plot to keep me there as a live specimen, kept in a virtual glass dome for training purposes. In Harefield Hospital's HDU, there was a woman whose head was encased in a large goldfish bowl. One of the unlucky ones, I thought, a woman with a rare diagnosis who has been captured for posterity. Sooner or later, I expected there to be a sign on the magnetic board above my bed: "Do not release this patient". Through days and days of waiting, my thoughts began turning to Tom Hanks' in the Terminal — left alone in an airport, eventually living there and becoming part of terminal life. Was this to be my lot? A lifetime living in a ward, the longest serving D bay patient, eventually people would forget why I was there and where I was going. I would eat, drink, shower each day, then start doing odd jobs, then be given a uniform, then one day, 10 years in the future, a TV company would come and film me and I would become a celebrity on The One Show.

A Is for **Accents**

Never one to shy away from a coffee at one of our established chains of high street coffee shops, I am always nervous of battling my way past the counter staff, who are inevitably of Eastern European origin and whose accent gives an edge to even the simplest of questions and gives the impression that if you do not answer them correctly and instantly, they will kill you. They fire questions at you about drink in or take out, size of coffee (reply must be in Italian), what extra shots and what food is required in a clear attempt to off balance you and reduce you to a quivering wreck, who will accept anything in the insulated, corrugated mug with the wrong initials on, that appears of the end of the process. So why is it that the same accents, when delivering instructions, administering words of comfort, asking for menu choices and asking whether you want just tea or coffee without all the extras, have a remarkably soothing effect, melting any preconceived stereotypes brought in from previous coffee shop disasters. Is it the situation, the fact that it is only single question at one time or the lack of a queue bearing down on you from behind with their answers to the questions preloaded into their heads? Maybe the coffee shop muddle is a middle-aged thing; perhaps, we middle-aged people should stick to women's institute coffee shops, where the only two questions are.... black or white and cake or no cake?

In the hospital, there was a real diverse mix of people—from Philipino, Portuguese and West Indian nurses to Pakistani, Polish and English patients. With so many accents, some of the conversations, therefore, take a strange and circuitous route. It is as if lots of questions have been written out on bits of paper, put in a bingo tumbler machine and the answers written out and put in a separate machine. During a conversation, they are then pulled out like teams being drawn for the FA Cup matches.

Question: "Where are you from?"

Answer: "10 years."

Question: "How long have you been in the UK?"

Answer: "Constipation."

It begs the question that how does anything get recorded correctly and medication administered correctly when no one can understand each other?

Answer: "Lithuania."

B Is for **Beds**

People will tell you that NHS beds are uncomfortable, too hard or too soft and too hot and sweaty. In a nutshell, I can confirm that they are right. Beds are essentially functional items with an additional (dis)comfort factor of a rubber-coated mattress added as an afterthought. But underneath that surface stereotype rubber-coated mattress lies a complex mechanical monster that has to be able to be wheeled around (with patients on board), bent into all positions, raised, lowered and act as a bed and as a trolley. Being in hospital for some time, I undertook a study of the beds around me. In my bay alone, there were four different types from the grand sounding Formula One style Enterprise 8000 that my fellow inmate had across the way from me, with control panels built into the side guards, to the less grand sounding Enterprise 5000 that I had, with a simpler, tubular construction side guard and single control panel on the end. Another inmate had a Nimbus 3, which had a life support pack attached to it. Harry Potter would have been proud of a Nimbus 3 bed instead of a Nimbus 2000 broomstick. All bed types allow the patient to stretch out flat or contort themselves into a position that a yoga teacher would be proud off. You could literally fold yourself in two, although it is probably not recommended.

All beds have levers for locking the wheels, locking the bed in position and releasing and locking the side panels. And most Harry Potter like of all, hospital beds have a knack of being able to shrink in width; without that magic ability, I swear that the porters and nurses would never get them through the doorways and corridors filled with nurses, cabinets, frames, tea trollies, lost visitors and men sent looking for chairs and vacant toilets.

There is a wide range of bed designs to spot and identify, maybe there should be an I Spy book of hospital beds, like the lists of train carriage numbers, we sat on bridges and ticked off years ago. It worried me that I found bed construction and design so interesting, I guess this is my brain working on the boredom aspect. How could I ever be jealous of someone else's bed? But why will I never forget the Enterprise 5000?

The heat of the ward and the coating of the Pentaflex Premium rubber mattress encourage sweating during the night. Seeing the results in the morning, led me to solve the mystery of the Turin Shroud. It is very likely that the Turin Shroud, holy relic of the Christian church and said to have the imprint of Christ stained on it, is actually an NHS bed sheet with an imprint of the sleeping Mr Symonds from Macclesfield. Although I tried, I could not recreate the Jesus image, all I could manage was a blurry head stain from my bald head and a small skid. Maybe it needs a few days of lying comatose to give the stain some definition. The original creator of the Turin Shroud must have considered a small skid unnecessary to authenticate a sheet from someone of the stature of Christ.

B Is for **the Bristol Stool Chart (and Other Useful Charts)**

At the time of writing, my daughter lived in Bristol, and I know the city of Bristol is famous for many things. It is famous for being the home of great Brunel feats of engineering such as the Great Western Railway, the SS Great Britain and the Clifton Suspension Bridge. It is famous for being the location of BBC series "Being Human" and Channel Four's hit series "Skins". It is famous for two sieges in the English Civil War in 1643 and 1645. It is famous as the home of band, Massive Attack, and for being the home of artist Banksy. It is probably famous for many other things that I haven't mentioned, but not many people in Bristol will know that Bristol gives its name to the Bristol Stool Chart—the standard hospital chart for the measurement of shit. Clearly, the inventor of the stool chart (if inventing is the right word), Dr K.W. Heaton, had nothing better to do when he put this illustrated sheet of sausages, snakes, lumps and blobs together. He must have felt proud of his achievement. The chart categorises seven types of shit with pictures of each one; type one is constipation, type seven is diarrhoea. Weirdly, once you have studied the chart, you do start to rate your stools, is this another sign of institutionalisation? No wonder, Isambard Kingdom Brunel did a lot of work in Bristol but lived in Portsmouth.

I am not sure what it is about Bristol that organisations like to associate themselves with the city, although not base themselves there. There is a medication manufacturer called Bristol Laboratories Ltd, but they are based in Hertfordshire. There is another medical breakthrough that Bristol is sort of famous for, the wobbly over bed tables and other hospital furniture. I will comment on the tables later but they are crafted by a blind man, who can't measure accurately, working for a company called Bristol Maid. Strangely, that company is based in Blandford Forum, so Bristol is a misnomer but any publicity is good publicity if you live in Bristol and you only have your stools to fall back on.

Whilst talking of scales, another interesting scale is the NHS pain scale, not illustrated like the poo chart, (although some versions seem to be inhabited by comic characters) but on a scale of 1 to 10. If you have never been in real pain before, it is difficult to define where you are on the pain scale. In some versions of the scale, they ask you to think of a time when you were in pain and use that to benchmark the scale. They use examples such as having a baby or having gallstones, which I have reliably heard are very painful things. I fell off my bike once when I was seven and grazed my knee, so I decided to use that as the midpoint in my pain scale. Then you can rate yourself and build your pain chart around your known pain. So, I decided a stinging nettle rash was worthy of one and worked up in pain from there.

1. 1—a stinging nettle rash, aged 5.
2. 2—a frozen lolly stuck to the tongue, remarkably painful, aged 10.
3. 3—the day I realised Hannah from SClub7 didn't love me in the same way that I loved her. Emotional pain hurts as well, aged 46.
4. 4—stubbed toe, never kick your sister in a rage when she wins at backgammon, aged 26.
5. 5—fell off my bike and grazed my leg on the stabiliser, aged 7.
6. 6—a misunderstanding with a French kiss, aged 12.
7. 7—a vasectomy, aged 39, thank you Valium!
8. 8—took a football in the nuts, aged 40.
9. 9—constipation, aged 8, aged 9, aged 12, aged 14, aged 14, aged 14 again (1977 was a bad year).

10. 10—went to the toilet after cutting chillies and not washing my hands first, aged 53.

You need the mental pain chart in your mind when you go into hospital. The nurse will ask you every day, "Are you in pain?" An affirmative answer then gets the response, "How do you rate your pain on a scale of 1 to 10?" According to medical opinion and not my own method of measuring pain, apparently: one is virtually nothing; seven-eight is verging on the unconscious; with nine, you can't tell the nurse you are in pain because you are in too much pain; and if you say 10, you are lying because you should be unconscious. There are not many 10s given out. I found that as well as being a scale for pain, this can also be adapted as a scale for rating one's ward mates.

1. 0—pain free, top guy, you would like to be mates on the outside, he is a good laugh, good conversation. You would trust him to put out your wheelie bins when you are on holiday.
2. 1—very minor annoyance—occasional snoring and moaning with pain, you still have sympathy with his condition, a positive guy, a high possibility you could be mates on the outside. If you were neighbours, it would be fine.
3. 2—minor occasional annoyance—sometimes makes you cringe but sometimes makes you laugh, will meet up now and again on the outside.
4. 3—annoying enough to be distracting, he talks too much, he keeps interrupting, could go either way on a night out.
5. 4—distractingly annoying—he can be ignored if you concentrate on pretending to ignore him, but he is still distracting, pretty sure you will avoid him on the outside. You can live with him in small doses.
6. 5—just annoying—he can't be ignored for more than 30 minutes. He does not stop talking, he wants you to

have his phone number and keep in touch and you give him a number with digits in the wrong order.

7. 6—he can't be ignored for any length of time; he is argumentative, he is never happy, he is always negative, you wouldn't want to bump into him but you know you will.

8. 7—the constant wittering makes it difficult to concentrate, he drones on, his life interferes with your sleep, he has the TV on all the time, he is on the phone all the time, he uses his phone on speaker phone, he is very negative, he complains about everything, but he thinks you are his best mate. He would love to see you on the outside but the view is not reciprocated.

9. 8—doing anything or going anywhere without loud comment being passed is impossible. Nausea and dizziness may occur if he keeps on all the time. His booming or wittering voice could actually make you more ill. Pretend to be asleep all the time to avoid conversation, you will positively avoid him if you see him first in the street.

10. 9—completely irritating—the sound of his voice makes you want to pass out or do yourself in. He is not on your Christmas card list. He is probably not on many Christmas card lists.

11. 10—he never gives up. His presence and constant rambling wants you to commit murder. He thinks that he is God's gift to the nurses and he thinks that he is the funniest man in the hospital. You never want to see him on the inside, let alone meet up with him on the outside.

I had a treadmill test at the hospital. I am not a runner, let alone a walker on a treadmill; I had never walked on a treadmill before or even been close to one. I had been in a hospital bed for five weeks. I had no muscle definition left in my legs. The men in charge said that they would start slowly and build up speed. Go at your own pace, they said, just hold the bars and walk normally. They hauled me off after less than

30 seconds. I'm not sure if it was the ungainly stamping of my feet as they tried to keep up with the rest of my body, which was clinging onto the bars, or the look of surprise on my face when the treadmill started moving and I didn't that made them call a halt so quick, but it was over before I had really got started. Perhaps my mind was already distracted by the exertion scale they had given me to read prior to the test. I was going to be using this scale during the test, a scale I never got to put to the test. When I had the treadmill test, I was asked to read off the Borg Exertion Scale—a scale numbered 6 to 20, where 6 to 11 is light exertion, 12 to 15 is medium exertion and 16 to 20 is hard exertion. I am not sure what happened to numbers 1 to 5; maybe in Sweden, they don't have one to five in their numbering system or one to five is couch potato, end of the scale and therefore, irrelevant. I assumed, falsely as it turned out, that this scale was from a tennis training camp set up by Bjorn Borg, the Swedish tennis player (never assume there is only one Borg in Sweden, it is a common Swedish name), but it was actually invented by Gunner Borg (also Swedish), a kinetics doctor from Stockholm University in 1998. He is on LinkedIn, still working with his wife at inventing scales today and giving lectures on exertion around the world. I wonder if his whole life is based on a building block of scales. Where we would have plaques in our homes of house rules and man cave rules, his house is probably full of scales, the Borg scale of how tasty my dinner was, the Borg scale of how well my wife drives, the Borg scale of strength of coffee and so on. I wonder if he uses the Bristol Stool Chart or if he has made up a stool chart of his own?

I will try and attend one of his lectures one day and then I can rate him on a scale of 1 to 10; I think he would see the funny side of that, as long as he does not want any treadmill volunteers.

C Is for **Consultant**

Each morning, "the team" come around the ward and into each bay. The consultants and doctors are identified by the stethoscope they have hanging around their neck like their badge of rank. No uniform is required to identify a consultant, the stethoscope speaks for itself like a mayor just has to wear a chain. They take away the folders, reading through your notes, then return to envelope their patients in the voluminous concertina curtains and talk the language of medicine, which is alien to any patient unless they happen to have been trained for four years at medical school. After 10 minutes of straight talking, they ask if there are any questions and then leave. They always have a house officer with them who then comes back with the interpreted version for the hard of hearing, hard of understanding and normal people. As I found out when they came to give me my diagnosis, you only hear certain bits of the conversation, usually the bits you weren't expecting to hear such as invasive surgery, mortality rate, three months off work. The words and sentences that join those key phrases together are lost as the key points bounce around inside your head like someone has just pushed a cricket ball into your head through your ear. Then there are phrases such as baseline mobility, lifestyle change and for the rest of your life. They talk to each other in a language with words that end in tones, tenes, nols, phols, prils and tins. Consultants should come with subtitles or translation as standard and very big name badges. I could not remember the names of any of the consultants who came around to see me without asking a nurse afterwards.

C Is for **CTU and HDU**

After any operation, you —the patient—will find yourself in CTU (Critical Trauma Unit) and then HDU (High Dependency Unit) prior to a trip back to a ward. These are basically monitor storage rooms with fancy names and you are conveniently dumped amongst all these monitors with other patients, while the anaesthetic wears off. The rooms could be a PC World store's back storage room, or they could actually be the rooms where the hospital's IT crowd live, but no one knows what is behind the rows of monitors and cables. They could also be well-disguised spy rooms, where the monitors tracking the world's greatest villains are powered by human organs and suck the life and knowledge from human brains. CTU was in darkness or so it seemed, it was like the flight deck of the Starship Enterprise. Back to reality, these rooms are where you get back to some sort of normality before returning to the ward for the rest of your stay. Your stay here is normally brief but you will not remember much about it because of the general anaesthetic wearing off, which can lead to some brutal hallucinatory dreams. This adds to the mystery of the visit —was I really there, who was there, where is it? You have the most individual service from a nurse who is tracking all your vital signs on a computer and watching them on an individual monitor; either that or she is watching series five of Game of Thrones for the third time whilst checking your blood pressure, temperature and oxygen level every four hours but pretending that she is a coiled spring, ready to jump into action at a moment's notice.

HDU and CTU are very similar but HDU is more like a ward. This is where you are a bit more aware of what is going on and you can have more visitors. This is also the point where those patients who want to scrounge off the NHS forever have their first opportunity to create diversionary tactics. After HDU, it is back to a ward and usually home within a week, but if you manage to fall or slide to the floor dramatically from your bed, you can start a chain of events that can keep you in hospital for weeks.

C Is for **Curtains**

These are the concertina plastic or flowing cloth curtains that are used to protect your modesty and privacy, although they don't particularly succeed in either capacity. When I was in one hospital, they had just replaced the old curtains with new corporate blue ones held into their track with plastic tabs. I think they were designed as quick release because every time they were closed, some of the corrugated blue fabric fell from the tabs. Everyone under six-foot-tall seemed to have trouble opening and closing them and once they surrounded a patient, there were always gaps where two curtains joined. Doctors and consultants would swan into the bay, pull the curtains awkwardly round the patient, do their medical talk bit and then leave the bay with the curtains still surrounding the patient; the nurses then spent time pulling them all back, making them tidy and re-attaching the corrugations to the tabs. I think the doctors thought that the new curtains had mysterious powers of absorbing sound, as they would talk to patients behind them as if nobody else could hear. In fact, the rest of the bay were silent, listening intently to the latest diagnosis. Cloth or plastic curtains made no difference to sound absorption or privacy, but the cloth curtains could be opened by a patient reaching out an arm even while lying on his Enterprise 8000 bed. Why has no one considered adding a button to the beds that would automatically open and shut the curtains? Maybe that is on the luxury Enterprise 12000.

The curtains were also designed to provide a physical barrier between you and the next patient at intimate moments. The intimate moments for the people next to me usually occurred when I was eating, which was often. I have sat and eaten my Chinese sweet and sour chicken and my chicken curry; whilst a thin slither of fabric separated me from the sights, smells and sounds of nurses giving enemas, nurses giving bed baths, patients peeing into papier-mâché vessels, patients farting and bed accidents being cleared up. You learn during your confinement that eating is more important. You can blot out the farts, the groans, the running pee and the nurses running commentary about cheesy willies and still enjoy the benefits of a rhubarb crumble and custard.

I will probably not eat rhubarb crumble and custard on the outside ever again.

D Is for **the Discharge Nurse and Going Home**

What a job of power in a hospital. Your job is to release people from their agony and restore hope that a trip home is just around the corner. As you walk up the ward corridor, all the patients look at you with expectant smiles whilst trying to read the name on the bit of paper in your hand. You can smile back and play cruel games like making eye contact briefly before carrying on past. "Pick me," someone shouts, "I'm Spartacus!" says another, picked up by the rest of the ward. One person gets the golden ticket and for them, life in the institution is over. Like demobbing from the army, or leaving prison, they are about to be exited into the outside world.

In the hospital I was in, the discharge nurses wore green uniforms, the green of hope and green for GO! They smiled a lot and joked with me about how well I looked when I went for exercise around the ward corridor. But I never got a piece of paper that said I looked well enough to leave.

After the discharge nurse has tempted you with her bit of paper, checked that you can get home, warned you of the changes in the big wide world such as the new mobile phones and the dangers of noiseless electric cars and then checked that your relatives will remember you and you have filled in the ward rating survey and your property check list, she utters the words that will come to haunt you for the next few hours. "Pharmacy will be up with your medication shortly, then you can go home."

Something I constantly worried about, while I lay in hospital and time moved slowly on, was at what point my relatives and friends would say, "John who?" After some time, would life at home just slip into a new era naturally, where the house remains tidy all the time, the shopping bill is less and the moaning would be forgotten? Cobwebs would form in the loft and the shed. Football would never come on the TV and my wife could watch Neighbours and Death in Paradise on TV without anyone making sarcastic comments next to her. My family visits to the hospital would shrink from daily to every other day, to weekly, then my family would forget why they were going out each night. Communications would stop. Neighbours at home would wonder at first if I was being secretly imprisoned underground in some cellar like chamber or chopped up and put in the brown wheelie bin marked garden waste but then they would forget to think about it. My mother would be first to forget my existence; at 91, she can't remember back more than a week so after a week of me being in hospital and no shopping appearing on the door step as if by magic, she would resolve with herself that the last 50 years were a bad dream and life, although in a leaner, hungrier format could start again. My dad, who had just failed a dementia assessment when I went into hospital, would be more concerned about shuffling old letters into a new pile and reciting each and every registration plate of every vehicle he drove in World War II. My in laws would be next—much more with it, they would need no encouragement as they have tried to forget I existed before and only needed an opportunity as an excuse to instantly forget my existence. They would then encourage their daughter to do the same. The cost of the hypnosis sessions would be considered worthwhile. And so, down the family chain it would go until my 20-year old son would be down the pub telling everyone that he never knew his dad, that he went overseas when my son was young and never returned.

E Is for **Entertainment**

What is the definition of entertainment? In the first hospital I stayed in, "entertainment" had a different meaning from entertainment in other establishments including HM prisons, the Trident carrying submarines hiding somewhere six miles down at the bottom of the ocean and the international space station. When I say different meaning, I would rather stuck on a space station than in a ward at a hospital when it comes to be being able to watch something. The lack of entertainment available was probably the only complaint I had of the care I received. There was a certain amount of free entertainment on the TV—four hours of BBC, ITV, Channel 4 and Channel 5 from 08.00 to 12.00. This had a few issues. You could watch the news but you only caught the end of the news when they have the feel good stories, the weather (which was irrelevant to me) and occasional mention of the headlines. On Sunday, you can watch Match of the Day but you miss the first half an hour when they play the highlights of the most exciting games, and you join it when they are onto the low scoring games and the feature on Match of the Day on Sunday about local community work. On a weekday, the time between 09.00 and 12.00 is filled with Lorraine, Good Morning Britain, Jeremy Kyle, Homes Under the Hammer, Can't Pay? We'll Take It Away!, Heir Hunters and other repeats of programmes that are over 10 years old. When you want to be lifted in spirits and have your brain taxed, 08.00 to 12.00 is the worst time of the day. After 12.00, you can watch more TV but you have to pay. I objected that in 2018, you have to pay to watch 10-year-old repeats, tacky game shows and other trash that populates the main channels. After five weeks of watching nothing, my second hospital home had free TV. I watched repeats from 10 years ago, tacky game shows and loads of other trash and wondered... what is the point of resisting? My neighbour in the bed next door had repeats of The Chase on a loop from 08.30 in the morning until 22.00 at night. Then proceeded to sleep most of the day.

At least radio was free in my first home, I thought optimistically that at least something is free until I saw the list of channels: Radio 2, Radio 4, Hospital radio and local radio. If you want to listen to some evening football, you can't do it on the radio because Radio 5 Live is not on the list, or you can pay best part of 30 pounds for three days access to the TV. Consequently, unless you want to give in to the paymasters, you are effectively cut off from the world, which, on the positive side, does encourage conversation and social interaction and gives the visiting relatives something to tell you about.

As entertainment from the TV and radio is limited without paying a fortune, entertainment has to come in other forms. One of these is a trip across the hospital for a test, another is a trip to another hospital for a special scan or procedure.

When I went to Harefield for an MRI scan, I went in an ambulance with attendant nurse as a date and a packed lunch for company. It was like a date and a day out rolled into one. A crap choice of date location to be fair and she had picked my least favourite crisps for the pack lunch, but I agreed to give her a good rating on hospital Tinder and swipe right for her. Or left, I can't remember.

F Is **the Fight for the Toilets**

There are four toilet/shower rooms on the ward for 30 patients and therefore, despite the fact that many of the 30 patients are immobile, there is a degree of competition for time in the toilet. However, I, as a comparatively mobile patient at the time, felt that I was always going to get space as over half the remaining patients could not move out of bed. But one man made it his life's work to scupper the plans I had for toilet domination. He was a small, very old man, who always lived in his pyjamas and walked only with the aid of a push along frame. His bay door was opposite my favourite shower room. The first hint I had that there was going to be some competition was when he saw me coming down the corridor with my wash bag, clothes and towel and smiled at me as he entered the shower room, shut the door and locked it with a satisfactory turn of the lock. I knew he was smiling on the other side, possibly even jumping around with delight, out of sight of the nurses who he had convinced that he was unable to walk unaided. Later on that morning, he slowly passed the entrance to my bay whilst on a walk and looked at me and smiled. That smile convinced me that he was up to no good and sure enough the next morning, as I left my bay, the metallic feet fitted with their rubber shoes appeared from his bay followed by his head. He glanced right, smiled and headed across the corridor to the shower. I swear to this day, he sped up. The frame made an impressive barrier; other than kicking it from under him, I could not get past him and he knew it. This event happened a few times, too many to be random, and each time his victory was followed by the walk of victory down the corridor past my bay. I considered cutting a leg off his frame at night and then listen for the crash or smearing the floor with butter that I could save back from two or three breakfasts, but in the end, I gave him the victory in the smug knowledge that I would be out of there before him. He went home the next day, whilst I cried on the sleeve of the smiling discharge nurse who commented how well I looked.

F Is for **Farting**

Le Pétomaine was the stage name of the French flatulist (what a great name for a professional farter) and entertainer, Joseph Pujol, who was famous for his remarkable control of the abdominal muscles which enabled him to seemingly fart at will. He was played by the late great Leonard Rossiter in the film of the same name. However, breaking wind is still socially unacceptable in some circles; while in other cultures, farting and belching are seen as normal. As my mother has said many times, and she practices what she preaches (and may well have been in the film credits as technical advisor), "Better out than in." But my mum never really moved in social circles that may have given her a hint that exhausting gas from her backside with an orchestral accompaniment was, in any way, socially unacceptable. Now at 90, it is irrelevant as her backside has developed a mind of its own and she is incapable of controlling any movements or sound, let alone organising them into a coherent concert. And so, the better out than in belief filtered down to us children and led to some embarrassing moments in our formative years. And what is the origin of the phrase "more tea, vicar?" which some people exclaim after a particularly noisy fart?

Farting is a normal bodily function that at my house has become a type of sad art form performed with the intention of making people laugh. However, when I am in company or out with people, I have grown to know the etiquette and either supress all urges or fart silently and then move somewhere else and look back with surprise at where I was standing. I know that silent farts on hard chairs are difficult but soft cushions will absorb the vibrations. Professional farting is all about redirecting blame.

So, what to do in hospital? I started just breaking wind gently and keeping it silent, but a man opposite me went full throttle from the word go. He was on laxatives and I was worried that he would fart one day and fire himself around the bay like a full balloon let go by a careless child until he ran out of gas and collapsed as skin somewhere in the room. However, no one looked concerned or even stifled a snigger, although I was concerned that the rest of us may suffer, as well as the poor gentleman's pyjamas. Maybe farting is acceptable in hospital, or even expected; I did get more reckless after this incident leading to occasional outbursts unexpectedly. I heard myself saying, "Better out than in," and, "More tea, vicar?"

F Is for **Friends, Family and Visitors You Want to See**

Many years ago, NHS visiting time was strictly enforced and restricted to an hour or two at the most. Numbers of people were restricted and any potential rowdy element was thrown out by the matron and their names put on a board of the banned. Sitting on a bed was severely frowned upon. Patients were checked for any sign of tiredness and at the first signs of a droopy head, everyone was out. In recent times, these practices have been replaced by a much more relaxed visiting structure on most wards, leaving the onus on the visitor to decide when they are going to go and leading to some awkward silences and conversations. A visual assessment of visitors can be a good indication of why the actual patient is in the cardiac ward—they, and what they bring in, are an indicator of the lifestyle, diet and exercise regime employed at home.

At first, visitors are always jolly, they come bearing gifts and their body temperature is still on a par with the outside world and has not yet adapted to the tropical ward temperature. They smile awkwardly at other patients and their visitors and say hello. They have a bond, they have never met before and may never see these people again, but they are all visitors and so they feel they can talk to each other. Women particularly will start talking, discussing all aspects of the patients and their time in hospital. Men nod heads and raise eyebrows in greeting to other men, then stand awkwardly, looking for a clock and reminding themselves of the time on the car parking ticket.

Visitors are always overcome by some magnetic field that affects their balance and sense of direction. Clothing is caught on chairs, bags tangle with the equipment on the end of the bed and there is this desire to bunch up and bump into each other as they approach the bed. Coats come off and bags are emptied of gifts and essentials. The men folk undertake the tasks they were designed for back in caveman days—the hunter gatherer instinct: chasing down any vacant chairs; going to the shop to get coffees and teas and papers; before standing around, awaiting further orders; reading the papers; checking football scores and BBC news on their phones. Smalltalk is not a man's game, so after hearing the lurid details of any operations and making the usual (but in 2018, inappropriate) jokes about nurses in uniform, conversation can generally dry up.

Women like to know more about the basic needs. Have you slept OK? What is the mattress like? Do they change bedding each day? Have you showered today? Are you regular? What is the food like? Have you lost weight? Have you drunk enough? There must be a Dorling Kindersley pocket guide to visitor's questions available that you can fill in on each visit. They will keep mental notes of all the answers, because they will have to regurgitate these numbers to other family members and women friends that they will meet, who will ask the same list of questions, while their husbands quip about nurses and uniforms.

Outside of the ward, there has already been a conversation between the visitors on how long they will stay and what is the trigger for leaving. "We won't stay long" is often the first comment made, the leaving time is now open. "Time we made a move" or "Right, we'll leave you in peace" is the code for get your coat on.

Allowing the use of mobile phones has made a big improvement to the visiting experience. When mobile phones first came out in the 1980s, they were banned in hospitals because they could upset the equipment. And no doubt, in those days, the giant bricks of unshielded electronics and the accompanying bomb of a charger could have been a viable risk. They were banned at petrol pumps allegedly because they could cause an explosion but that has never been proven to be a real risk. Despite there still being a big sign at the ward entrance reminding mobile users of the same thing, clearly there is not the same level of concern that pressing send and sending a selfie taken at someone's bedside will cause cardiac failure to some unsuspecting person attached to an ECG or defibrillator further down the ward. I think the modern practice of dividing wards into smaller bays has been a satisfactory compromise to negate the risk. A phone call from an old-style phone ordering a pepperoni pizza can now only wipe out only four instead of twenty-four. Again, in 2018, there is more concern about any inappropriate use of the pictures or the phone, rather than the medical effect it has on 90-80 year olds two beds down (unless they are in the background of your selfie, dancing on the tables). Everyone uses mobile phones all the time without questions being asked; it allows patients to remind visitors of what to bring, allows some scheduling of appointments to avoid awkward visitor overlaps and also allows the visitors to be able to while away those commonly awkward moments when the patient is either asleep or the conversation dries up. When friends and family bring things, it is good to be specific with the mobile phone instruction; otherwise they bring in things that in any other situation, they would not have considered buying you, especially in the magazine and sweet categories.

Top ten visitor's brought items (in no particular order), you can tick these off after each visit.

Electrical items (any one of mobiles, tablets, chargers, laptops, headphones): Vital communications in the modern world of hospital life.

Sweets and snacks: Still popular to bring in the sweets of the *visitor's* choice—pastilles, chocolate (that instantly melts into a soft mud texture like substance that squeezes apart rather than breaks) and (and I don't know why) Werther's Original and Fox's Glacier Mints. Maybe you're suddenly meant to like these types of sweets in hospital when you have never shown an interest in the past. There is an assumption amongst even closest friends that you become someone different in hospital. You are now not the person from the outside but the patient and because of that, all tastes have changed. Sweets, like newspapers and magazines, are the currency of friendship on the ward. If you are allowed, crisps are a tempting snack because they bring some crunch to the mouth; most hospital food is not crunchy, so a mouthful of crisps can be a luxury like no other.

Spare clothes: It is nice to get dressed every day even if you are not going anywhere. No snoozing in onesies or lying around in pyjamas, slovenly behaviour should not be encouraged!

Toiletries: Smelling nice in hospital is important, maintaining bodily odour is vital to self-respect and gaining the respect of your bay mates. Contrary to popular opinion, the nurses don't care what you smell like, your Lynx and Packo Roban musky smells won't impress them.

Books, Puzzle books, Arrow words, Sudoku books and Crosswords: You receive endless puzzle books and especially Sudoku books. It is worth learning how to do these number puzzles before you ever have to go into hospital or be in any boredom situation as they can while away hours very easily. Vary your arrow wordbooks, how many times does (Omar) Sharif, the title of the Bishop of York (Ebor) and (Enzo) Ferrari turn up as clues in the same book.

DVDs: With all the live streaming going on, I was under the impression that DVDs were a thing of the past, but in hospital, with no WIFI, they are a godsend. But don't forget to text your visitors which ones you want, why would a man in his 50s want to watch Disney? It is strange how your close friends and family, who should know your taste in movies, when left to their own devices, will appear with bags of DVDs that they feel will make good hospital viewing but which will have little or no impact on the anti-boredom factor. I was tasting everything from Sylvester Stallone gun fests to Star Trek Beyond (any recognition from how I remember it) to cartoon animals. One could say that it broadened my horizon (especially Star Trek as it took me boldly where no filmgoer has gone before) but, in fact, it narrowed my cinematic taste even further.

Also have something to play DVDs on!

Newspapers and magazines: Newspapers are vital if you do not have access to TV. But don't say no to them even if you have got access to TV. They are also the currency of friendship on ward bays.

Fruit: The old joke about coming in with grapes still applies, it seems, and every table is immediately decorated with a satsuma as soon as a patient is installed but of course, in the modern world, there is an awful lot more choice of healthy foods to bring in, all free of something—almost all free of taste.

Drink: Robertson's Real Fruit Barley drink, Lucozade, fruit drinks, orange juice, various waters. Staying hydrated in the tropical heat of the ward is important and there may be fluid restriction rules depending on your condition. As I found out, however, if you are on tablets to reduce water retention, don't over drink. Water tablets make you want to pee out of the pores of your skin.

Top 10 visitor's comments: To play this game, you must get the visitor to ask the following questions or make the following comments.

How are you? The classic opening line. Although tempted to answer with "not great, have you noticed I'm in a hospital", one should always be optimistic enough to say "yes, I'm fine". Any other answer will be interpreted as a sign of weakness and will lead to discussions on your mental health fragility on the way back to the car. This opening line has multiple opportunities for banter, jokes and the odd, serious comment and has to be the number one useful visitor's comment for getting the party started.

At least you're in the right place: Essentially true but not by choice, the right place for me by choice would be a pub by the coastal path in Cornwall, not a hospital bed D1 in the cardiac ward, the NHS.

There will always be someone worse off than you: And there is nowhere like a hospital for making that comment. It does not always seem right but that comment is seriously a great leveller.

It's hot in here: Everywhere in a hospital is steaming except corridors, lifts and cafés, which are always cold. Scanning rooms are cold but they have to be temperature controlled, ward beds are plastic with a memory imprint of your body shape imprinted in sweat. When a patient is changed, the nurse strips the bed of all bedding and then uses a magic spray to remove the memory imprint.

On the subject of beds and bedding, one of the things to look forward to at Hotel NHS is a clean sheet every night. Crisp, clean sheets are tucked in each day in an attempt to make the most uncomfortable beds in the world inhabitable. By the next morning, after a night of sweating, tossing and turning and being woken up, the sheets lie as wrinkled as the face of a very old man.

We won't stay long: The ones you want to stay never do, they are too aware of the rules of visitation (and they have also studied in detail the car park charges); the ones that are OK in short doses will always say that they can't stay long but will stay forever until either the sweets run out, the awkward silences get too much or the heat drives them off.

Do you need anything? In other words, we need an excuse to go out for a while and get away from the heat in the ward.

You look well: The standard start to a conversation when there is little else to say. We all know, I don't but, it makes you feel better for them to have said it.

Weather Report: Only the British talk about the weather so much and having someone trapped in a ward, without access to the outside world, gives the visitor an opportunity to provide an hour-by-hour report on the weather conditions. Without seeming ungrateful for these updates, the only reports I am interested in are related to my body fluids and bodily functions.

Home report: This is more like conversation—the reports of how people are in the outside world, what has happened and who has done what. These reports make you feel included and still part of something other than just merging slowly into the hospital fabric.

Bonus questions: You can make up bonus questions that you have to try and make the visitors ask. These could be different for different visitors. If the question is successfully asked, you can have a bonus point.

Once the visitors have exhausted you with the standard questions and any bonus questions, and once they have told you all about their recent holidays in the sun and their plans for the weekend, it is time for them to leave; except for one lady visiting the guy opposite me, who sat there knitting all the time she was there and after he had fallen asleep thinking that she was going. It must have been a particularly important knitting project, and she must have felt the quiet visiting hours gave her time to get the project finished, very resourceful. By the time the visitors leave, the small cupboard for personal effects is crammed with stuff and the strip of narrow table now has piles of things to sort through and shuffle around. I was convinced that my wife was emptying some of my possessions from the house each time she came, and that when I went home, there would be no evidence that I ever existed. The only reason I was being kept in the hospital was that my wife had bribed the nurses to keep me here; whilst she completed the brain washing on my children that taught them to forget who I was. I seemed to have more possessions than anyone else on the ward. My wobbly cantilever table was overloaded, my little cupboard bursting and my non-comfy cushioned chair similarly stacked. But then, I had been there longer than anyone else. When I moved wards after the first week, I disappeared under a heap of carrier bags of possessions.

When I was in the cardiac ward, my bay of four go to know each other quite well. Relatives started bringing cakes and muffins on Sunday afternoons and handing them around to everyone, which was a welcome break from the usual food. One Sunday afternoon, some visitors gave an impromptu jive dancing session. I couldn't help asking myself the question though, four men with heart problems and the hospital does not restrict the eating of very full fat cakes? Is this long-term planning for job security by the cardiologists or a secret plot by all the relatives to finish us off?

After the first couple of weeks, the visitors realise that this could be a long haul and the visits start to dry up, except for the die-hard relatives, whose duty is to come each day and sit reading, sleeping or forcing you to do more word searches. The outside world gets further out of reach and the institution sucks you further in, like the TARDIS getting sucked into a time warp. I am not sure after what time period staying in a hospital, you need rehabilitation before you leave, and how long before the world has moved on so far that you will not be able to fit back into society.

In true NHS style, a chart can be used to re the visitor experience, in terms of what rewards they should be entitled to.

1. Very frequent visitors, outstanding visitor value, worth a four-course meal out at a nice restaurant. These visitors will ask if they can do anything for me. Applying moisturiser to my feet was my standard test for visitors. Any visitor willing to put their hands on the line for that job will always be a one on my scale.
2. Regular visitors, put themselves out, worth at least a nice meal out.
3. Infrequent but respectfully regular, a good takeaway.
4. Didn't have to come, not tied to commitment by family ties, put themselves out to come, worth coffee and cake.
5. Occasional visits, expected visits, check they are still on the Christmas card list.
6. Never came, off Christmas card list, this can divide families, where you are forced by reference to the scale to send a Christmas card to only one member of a family when one visited but the other didn't.

Before rating your visitors on the above scale, you need to take into account the visitors that come to see you on the outside during your recuperation as well as those who risked their immune system to come and see you on the inside. On the outside, some different visitors will appear clutching cakes and fruit, visits will be a bit longer and more relaxed. Visitors are just as important after release as during confinement, especially when the rest of the family have decided that you are now a phoney, playing the system and have all gone back at work.

F Is for **Food**

I was interned in a cardiac ward, the definition of cardiac is things related to the heart. Diet is always cited as one of those things. Some heart conditions come from lifestyle as I saw a few times with people passing through. The old adage of "eat less, exercise more" and "do not drink alcohol to excess" was never more of a true statement when it comes to heart disease. It was, therefore, to be expected that the hospital menu would be designed and prepared with that in mind; I prepared myself for the bland world of hospital food. How surprised I was then when I was allowed free reign of the very tasty food menu— from chicken curry, sweet and sour chicken, full roast, Caribbean Jerk chicken, Shepherd's pie, meatballs and pasta and deserts including sponge pudding, custard and rhubarb crumble. More surprises lay in store when I was interned in the country's centre of excellence for heart surgery; a menu like that of a hotel and a full English breakfast every Sunday. In fact, eating well was positively encouraged and the visitors turning up with grapes and satsumas for their patients was also encouraged to ensure a speedy movement of all this food through the system. So, visitors turning up with fruit, I can understand, and there was plenty of that on display on the wobbly tables.

Yet, despite all the good food on offer, I have seen (and participated guiltily in) unofficial pleasures of the stomach. I even had my own stash of crisps and chocolate and fruit pastilles. I don't know why I needed them but I found I was sneaking them out to eat like a naughty schoolboy, either at night or when the nurses were on hand over or in the dark after lights out. Maybe I feared confiscation of my contraband and possible solitary confinement. However, it was completely unnecessary to disguise a snack when I was presented by other blatant breaches of camp rules that were going on all around me. I am convinced that visitors think that their loved ones will starve in hospital or think that they will hate the food, so elaborate schemes are devised for bringing in additional supplies. An Asian man had a three-week stay with us and his family brought in food constantly, as well as his three meals a day; he had heated food flasks, fish and chips, MacDonald's and a host of tubs brought in. Little time was there to eat all he had during the day, so he would be up at night eating also. When it came to weighing time, he was lighter than all of us. A Polish man came in with a bag full of traditional Polish sausage (basically a fat sausage with a hint of meat) and a loaf of bread so dense that it resembled cake; other people had digestive biscuits and bags of sweets on obvious display. Another patient's children brought in white chocolate and lemon muffins drizzled in icing and handed them around to all (they were very nice). Cakes appeared on birthdays and everyone tucked in. Takeaways were not frowned on. One night, we tested the system by ordering pizza from Harefield Village, then walked into the village and collected them and brought them back in. No one seemed to mind, I wish we had not walked straight past the pub now!

G Is for **The Great Escape (and Other Films/Shows to Watch in Hospital)**

Here is a selection of films or TV shows to watch to help get you into the prison humour/hospital humour mood that is needed for survival.

The Great Escape: Steve McQueen keeps trying to escape but always ends up back in the camp. Lots of escape plans, tunnel and solitary confinement cliché jokes to use. Just replace the Germans with nurses and hope you are on a ward with a wood burning stove below, which you can start a tunnel. Every ward should have a scrounger, a forger, the cooler for the isolation of problem prisoners (actually the side rooms).

The Colditz Story: More escape tunnel clichés and escaping from your captor's jokes. Also, plans made from toilet roll inners, a construction project for the long-term inmates.

The Wooden Horse: You've guessed it, more tunnels, more Germans, more escape jokes.

Carry on Matron/Carry on Doctor/Carry on Again Doctor: The greatest of British innuendo comedy set against the background of what the NHS was like in the 1960s when it truly was the best health service in the world.

The Shawshank Redemption: A good film to study how to make a real escape and no stupid Germans in sight!

Porridge: If you run out of wartime escape terminology and the Shawshank Redemption is too heavy, then light-hearted prison humour is the next best comparison. Keeping things from nurses, hiding vital supplies, calling each other inmates and talk of exercise yards and scaling fences, it is like carry on in prison.

Try starting a sheet of how many clichés or escape related words you can use or hear people say while you are in hospital.

One Flew over the Cuckoo's Nest: Institution film about the comradery of inmates in a mental hospital.

G Is for **Gang Culture**

Nothing to do with Hells Angel style gangs but the gang of mates you form in the bay and the ward. Once you associate with your bed mates and you have bonded through the exchange of medical stories and the barter of newspapers and food, they become you mates, your wingmen. You become dependent on each other from making menu decisions for you when you are at scans or procedures to helping with things you cannot do and to generally share banter with. When someone new arrives and an old gang member has gone, you need to initiate the new man into the group. Sometimes, he is not easy to accept and you find yourself getting protective of the gang you have helped form. Is this all part of institutionalism, the Animal Farm or Lord of the Flies effect? Becoming an accepted part of the gang is through initiation— offering a paper, a sweet, a deodorant or sharing your statistics on blood pressure, pulse and previous operations. These friendships may be fleeting or long lasting but the important thing to get through the long hours is to have someone else to interact with; a shared problem is a halved problem is very true. The gang members will become a new circle of friends where conversation surrounds your common reason for being there; whether it is broken limbs, breathing difficulties or in my case, stents, tales of MRI and CT scans, angiograms and the statistics of heart disease. This is a new shift in life and life perspective, the fragility of the body now becomes more of an interesting conversation than the fragility of the current arsenal management. This is something I wasn't expecting to happen, what I have titled "life perspective re-arrangement", it comes as a shock to begin with. Arsenal will carry on winning or losing with different managers but life is a once only shot.

H Is for **Post-Op Hallucinations**

It must be a post-operative thing that the lack of sleep, the trauma to your body and mind, and the drugs produce a whole set of new dreams and images that play on your mind, like I imagine (with no experience to back up the claim) a good dose of magic mushrooms would do. Floating red settees, smiling cartoon dogs with pink hair, geometric block animals, painted trees, flashing images of vivid, multi-colours and images of little girls in polka dot raincoats disappearing into the wallpaper were common nightly themes for the first week after my operation. I stared at the TV screen above my bed one night and I was convinced that it had been burnt and the black plastic had gone into that crazed pattern that plastic does when it is burnt. I was so convinced that I got up in the morning, climbed on the bed and checked close up. The screen was fine and then I thought why am I checking this? The nurses that came to restrain me had seen it all before.

The weird hallucinations went on for about a week, along with weird dreams with everyone talking in French and Italian, like being involved in a Walter presents movie night on Channel 4 but without subtitles, then normality seemed to return.

H Is for **the History of Harefield Hospital**

Being a history lover, I have decided to add this brief interlude about Harefield Hospital because of the fascinating history it has. Harefield hospital is the world-famous heart hospital in the village of Harefield in West London. Do not be put off by the early 20th century exterior, or the fact that much of the inside is early 20th century too. It has the air of an old hospital from the corridors and folding doors to the interior ward fittings. It started life as a collection of shacks built as a hospital for the Australians in World War One and then became a Tuberculosis hospital. The current hospital was built and opened in 1937 with two curved "wings", each housing the patients facing the sun. It was chosen for a TB hospital because it was located high above sea level and therefore, considered to be good for hours of sun and fresher air, both of which at the time were considered good for TB. The curved wings face south and east to catch the best of the sun, whilst the corridors are on the north/west side. Patients were wheeled out onto balconies and into the garden to get the benefit of sun and air. In recent times, new buildings and extensions have been added and, sadly, most of the balconies have gone. From 1980, the hospital became associated with heart and lung transplants, the first of which was performed in 1983 by Sir Magdi Yacoub. Since then, it has become the centre for excellence in heart and lung research. The old-fashioned feeling and many original features of the hospital gives it a comforting feeling; my only hope during my stay was that the TB virus was not lurking in the walls under the paint and in cupboards, waiting to envelop unwary victims.

H Is for **Hospital Food and Nil by Mouth**

The hospital food I tasted was very good, the days of cold slop seem to be long gone in this modern world of patient come first front-line care. There was a menu of surprising diversity with good for you and no-good for you options. The three meals of the day become the framework around which all other things happened, to miss a meal was a small disaster. A major disaster is not being in the bay when the jolly catering lady comes and takes your order. Mealtimes are fixed points in time and everything else becomes measured in fractions of time between meals. Nothing else is as important as mealtimes. Visitors slot in between meals and all visitor conversation ends when food comes. Scans and procedures must be fitted in between meals. And although the opportunities for exercise are limited in hospital, you always seem hungry by the next mealtime. Maybe it is psychological anticipation, another pointer to the grinding effects of institutionalism or portion size or some drug added to the food to make you want more. Portion sizes are definitely smaller than you would receive at home, I don't mind admitting that more than once, I have looked at the uneaten dinner left by a sleeping or absent patient in the bed next door and wondered if it is inappropriate to take it. Only once did I actually take the meal from a man who had been discharged but his meal still came on the trolley, and I liked his choice so I had it after my own meal. I didn't consider that to be too wrong. I even considered asking if they do a takeaway service for non-patients for when I leave, I have got to like the food that much.

The worst scenario is to be told that you are nil by mouth until a procedure or scan. This can mean waiting all day with no meals. I have seen grown men cry uncontrollably when they have been nil by mouth all day and then a procedure is postponed. Not because the procedure is postponed but because they have missed a meal. Even the kind consoling words of fellow gang members cannot help with the grief in these situations. Better to close the curtains (if you can) and give the mate some time alone reflecting on chicken time they will never get back, sauce they will never taste and a rhubarb crumble and custard gone to waste. A boss told me once that time wasted can never be recovered. Lost meals can never be recovered, I am sure it is one of the main causes of depression in hospital along with missed tea opportunities and four free hours of Phillip Schofield and Jeremy Kyle.

I Is for **the Institution**

As I discovered when I entered the hospital initially and as I was then able to warn the "new optimists" about, as I called those that passed through the ward around me, you enter hospital with a plan in your head off when you are going to be out. After the initial trauma and time spent getting through A and E and then assessment, you are struck by the down to earth realisation that the hospital system has you logged and that, until they have exhausted all possible tests on you as a human being, some of them performed twice, there is no chance of a quick exit. It must have been the same feeling in August 1914 when World War One broke out and everyone was convinced that it would be over by the end of the summer and then by Christmas. When eventually it did end four years later, no one knew what to do, all that early optimism had been beaten out of them. And so, the same with the NHS, you go through the same declining optimism, could be out by tonight, could be out by tomorrow, could be out by the end of the week, it's only a couple of weeks.

I, very quickly, worked out that once you have a nametag with your allocated NHS number and patient number, you are into the system; then when you arrive on a ward, you can remain optimistic until your name is written on the board above the bed. At that point, it is not worth thinking ahead as life will become a routine of interminable waiting interspersed with bursts of, usually painful, activity (another similarity with the trench warfare of World War One). Doctors will come around and say all being well, you can go home tomorrow. But tomorrow never comes. They may mention Wednesday but that will become Thursday and Thursday will become Friday. Before you know it, a week will pass and then another week. Once it has all been battered out of you, you don't care what a doctor says; you can't believe him anymore. Doctors will always think that they are sowing some seeds of hope and happiness when they mention going home, but in all the people that passed before me, none went out in the first day or on the day they thought they were going to go. Then, at the moment you least expect it, the discharge nurse will appear brandishing her bit of paper and a broad smile.

What the discharge nurse does not warn you is that when you get home, you need to wean yourself off of institution life. The institution becomes deep rooted in you when you go home. Once you have experienced a few weeks of the same routine and then you get out and go home, you find it mentally difficult to return to normality. You are comforted by the beep of the cooker timer or the dishwasher finishing its cycle, they remind you of the monitors. I had to get my son to pull and open the curtains in the lounge regularly because they made the same sound as the hospital curtains. You wake up at the same time during the night for observations that never come. I wrapped a sock around my arm to give the comforting feel of the blood pressure cuff. Mealtimes need to be fixed in place. Floors feel colder and slippers don't shuffle the same on carpet. The piles of things have more space to be spread out on and then reshuffled. A satsuma and an arrow word magazine must be lying around.

I Is for **the IT Crowd**

Increasingly, hospitals are run by faster and faster computers that are designed in theory to talk to each other and act as mother databases for all hospitals to link up to. Press a button, fling out a patient's shoe size, life story, back story and, if you want to, medical records. This mother of all mother hubs is controlled usually by a couple of maintenance men, who live like moles burrowed into the system. Nurses ring for them, managers search for them, but, like a rare animal on Autumn watch, they will only emerge when they feel like it or they are smoked out. I only captured a rare glimpse of these animals once when the TV system on the ward broke and a riot nearly broke out. Out of the gloom emerged the IT men, who fancy themselves as the surgeons of the telemetry world. One, an individual Rasta with a massive, elongated beanie and the other with the phone and hence, identified as the main man in almost consultant casual dress. They dress like electrical consultants—for them, the stethoscope is replaced by coloured leads, the snappy dressing is replaced by an array of special screwdrivers and battery packs on their belts and doses in mg are replaced by amperages in ma. Steel toecaps and lightly dirty hands are the order of the day. People's lives rely on them, not sure if they actually know it.

K Is for **Kit List**

Thanks to my wife and her forward thinking, I came into hospital with a small bag of basic items. Many people come by ambulance and do not even have this basic kit. I developed my basic list into a list of must have items when entering hospital. Hopefully, there will be a relative or friend who can pack a bag for you and bring it in.

Pants: Always have spare underwear available, you never know when a skid might strike. Hospitals have not yet entered the aloe-vera-coated, deluxe quilted toilet tissue world, most of us now live in.

Leisure wear: As we now call it, that mix between pyjamas and lounge wear that is, both, decent and trendy. Otherwise, it is institution pyjamas, one size only, that fall down as you walk or make you trip over with the very long legs.

Shirts and trousers: I always maintained it is important to get up, get showered and dressed each day to make you feel human again.

Slippers: Shuffle slippers are an important badge of the inpatient.

Toiletries: Keep clean and smell nice, have moisturiser in abundance and lip salve for the cracked lips. The heat of the ward and the effects of medication can dry out the skin. Moisturise feet and hands every day or better get a friend, visitor or nurse to do it for you.

Couple of good books: These are not for long-term reading; starting to read a book always encourages sleep.

Sudoku book: Because everyone has one.

Standby Sudoku book: One to lay on your table whilst working on the other one.

Extreme Sudoku book: If you master Sudoku, this will give you some challenges.

Pad and pen: To make lists for visitors and for the point of making lists, for writing notes about the illness, records of conversations, phone numbers of new friends.

Fruit pastilles: Very satisfying to suck whilst doing Sudoku.

Tablet or some other item for entertainment: For watching movies or general internet.

Lucozade, Robinsons barley water: Because everyone has a bottle on their table.

Headphones: To plug into any device you might be watching or listening to.

Some change: In case there is a raffle to enter.

Some ear plugs: To blot out the noise from other people's devices when they have forgotten to bring their headphones and to blot out the noise of the ward at night.

Phone and charger: In the modern world, people are more interested in plug socket availability than their own condition.

K Is for **Keeping Regular**

Keeping regular is a prime objective when in hospital; each day, the nurses will ask if you have had a bowel movement or opened your bowels. Keeping mobile, eating your bodyweight in fruit each day and drinking orange juice, all help.

When constipation strikes, nurses get interested. There are a number of remedies that can be employed; the first is the equivalent of political sanctions in the form of Movicol—a light milk shake that gently moves things. If sanctions don't work, then a more severe reprimand is required. This is serious intervention and when I say intervention, I mean it. It involves a stick of dynamite inserted and put on a slow burn timer fuse. When it goes off, it is important to have the curtains closed around the victim to absorb the blast. You can usually tell that things are getting unstable when great, long, noisy farts start to emanate from the victim, who unfortunately has no ability to prevent or control the release. More tea, vicar!

L Is for **Life Re-Arrangement**

Life re-arrangement is all about what is going to happen next, once the operation is over. How are you going to approach life, has your experience changed your life and the way you approach life in general. It is a discussion you have with fellow inmates who are going through the same thing.

My first thought on getting home was should I have a midlife crisis. With time running out for me, to have one and now with this set back, should I buy a leather Stetson or a pimped-up motorbike? Live life to the full, live every day as if it is your last, hit life full on. Everyone talks about that after a major illness. Maybe dress more flamboyantly or go back to being a rock dude. Should I pursue my dream of becoming a successful Gigolo (another book)? Probably that was now unattainable as my Gigolo body was damaged.

I won't watch any more shite TV, I decided, life is too short to watch game shows, reality shows, antique shows, house buying shows. Unfortunately, for me, my first day out of hospital was spent watching Britain's Got Talent, First Dates, Bargain Hunt and Gogglebox. The family had deliberately recorded them so we could watch them together, which was thoughtful in a way. From one institution to another, maybe a few days like this before hitting life full throttle would be worthwhile. I just know that the full throttle life won't happen, maybe a gentle lift into third gear.

For me, every day is going to be a new challenge, I decided. No more coffee shops, no more shops, no more wasted time. Then on release day plus two, I found myself sitting in the car outside Dunelms; while my wife indulged in some much needed retail therapy.

I decided I would not moan as much now, I had had a life changing experience. However, on release day plus two, the BBC announced some new challenge shows—Britain's Best Home Cook with Claudia Winkleman, Britain's Best Garden Shop with Tom Kerridge, The Great Painting Challenge. Good old BBC, same old, same old.... and the winner is.... not me, I wrote and posted my first post-op moaning letter to the BBC's Head of Lack of Imagination.

Every day should include a good deed. My first good deed and the start of my life re-arrangement in action was to throw back, to the garden behind us, the footballs I had collected over the previous year from the boy, who used our fence as a goal and kept kicking balls over into our garden. After a frustrating time throwing them back, I decided to keep them and ended up with six of his footballs in my shed. So, I decided, life is too short to hold grudges with a seven-year-old and I threw them all back. A warm feeling of great satisfaction.

My new neighbour informed me that the family moved over the winter, and would I refrain from throwing balls into his garden or he would put them in his shed and keep them.

L Is for **Long Service Award**

In the world of industry, I inhabited before I was ill. Long service was recognised by the presenting of badges, usually tie pins, bottles of wine and silver-plated platters, all to the gentle applause of those work colleagues who could be bothered to come to the boardroom, tempted more by the light spread on offer than by the giving out of awards. I always felt, when I started work, that if I could make five years and get the tiepin, I would be proud of the fact that I would have made it in business. Yet I never had to wear a tie in the modern world of corporate work wear and tiepins looked ridiculous, attached to the lapels of polo shirts. At the same awards ceremony, an employee of 25 years' service was called the wrong name by her manager before he gave her one extra day of holiday per year. Polite applause over the munching of pizza slices and vol-au-vents. I wondered if she was now looking forward to 50 years' service and the next extra day holiday.

If you manage to stay in hospital long enough, you may be entitled to long service awards. My first long service award was a second pillow so that I could lay awake at night in more comfort. My second long service award was an extra towel so I could actually dry my whole body after a shower instead of drip-drying half of it. I don't know why the towels in the hospital were so small; they were slightly bigger than face flannels. I could ically only dry one leg with one and then I would stand near the heater to bake off the rest of the water.

My third long service award was an extra piece of toast, getting three rather than two. This was after three weeks in the ward. These long service awards were all more useful than a five-year tiepin.

L Is for **Lucozade and Other Energy Drinks**

Some people swear by the positive effects of energy drinks; others say they are all caffeine and sugar and clearly no good at all. Many years ago, when Lucozade first came out, the distinctive orange bottles used to be recommended by pharmacists and placed by helpful visitors on every hospital table as a means of providing a cheap gift on the basis that you need to be aiding your recovery after an operation. Lucozade has now become grouped in with the range of sports energy drinks like Red Bull and Monster rather than being marketed for its health-giving properties. The official NHS guidance on energy drinks is no too much caffeine and too much sugar. I did not see any of the modern, branded energy drinks in hospital, but I did see Lucozade, a testament to the fact that attempts at brand change is useless. Lucozade changed the slogan of the brand from "Lucozade aids recovery" to "Lucozade restores energy" in 1983. There are still a lot of people who think the first one applies.

M Is for **Mindfulness**

Mindfulness is meant to be a way of coping with stress by living in the moment. I have to be honest and say that I am a very sceptical person when it comes to mindfulness. That may surprise some people but not my close friends. Mindfulness goes in the same bucket as Feng Shui and Gluten Free in my view. People have made a lot of money by stating the bleeding obvious and charging people for their books that state the bleeding obvious in print. One of the things about mindfulness, that I am most cynical about, is the colouring books and, more particularly, the books full of blank pages with only a header as a title of something to draw. I am sceptical because they charge £13.99 for a book of blank pages that will probably never be filled in by the £8.99 pack of colouring pencils that are on the table next to the book. But maybe, faced with monotony and complete inescapable boredom, a drawing book could be a good idea. I never saw a man in hospital colouring in pictures, they were too busy filling in betting slips and sleeping mindfully. Maybe the women did more colouring in their bays. Every day in hospital is an opportunity for mindfulness, in fact, mindfulness was invented for hospital situations, where you really can forget about everything for a moment and dream of chewing raisins and skipping in the rain without being told to get back to work or being run over by a bus whilst feeling the tarmac on the soles of your feet as you cross the road. I have drawn up a list of possible titles for the blank pages of a hospital mindfulness book.

In the basic book, the headers could be actual objects such as a monitor, a table with things, a nurse, a hand sanitising station, a satsuma, a bowl of fruit, an Enterprise 8000 hospital bed, a man in a bed, a cupboard, a urine collection pot, a phlebotomist's trolley, a bottle of Lucozade, a full dinner plate, a tea trolley, a blood clot, a visitor, a get well soon card.

In the advanced book, the headers would be more mindful and test the imagination; titles such as optimism, clean sheet night, nil by mouth, a day out, hope, waiting, fluid restriction, the night before the op, the morning after, thirst, enema effect, into the unknown, family relationships, forgotten, baseline mobility, hospital silence, crushing dejection, lost optimism.

In the dot-to-dot version, the reader will be able to join the dots and make pictures of organs of the body including a detailed, labelled heart, lungs and kidneys, key equipment in a hospital, doctors and nurses (giving options for the impact of the uniform size guide).

N Is for **NHS**

The NHS is 70 years old this year. The NHS was born out of the ideal that good healthcare should be available to all, regardless of wealth. At its launch by Aneurin Bevan, the Minister for Health, on 5 July 1948, it had three core principles at its heart: that it meets the needs of everyone, that it be free at the point of delivery and that it be based on clinical need, not ability to pay. The great institution, we know as the NHS, was born out of World War 2 and its methods permeated down from hospitals through GP's to, inevitably, my mother. During the 60s and 70s, the wards were run by strict matrons, whose methods were the envy of parents the country over. My mother, in particular, showed far right maniac matron tendencies if I was ever off school ill. Her theory was that if I was treated like an inpatient with an infectious disease for the duration of the illness, then I would think twice and not be off sick very often—it worked. While other children had time off school, supposedly, sick and spent that time running around, having fun; I was placed in bed in our front downstairs lounge, which my mother had converted into an NHS ward replica. The camp bed frame she used is still in her loft as a monument to modern day torture and makes even the Enterprise 5000 look comfortable. I was allowed water and bed rest only until I was better, no television, which, when I think about my experience in modern times, was actually only a slightly worse fate than I experienced. I remember the GP coming around and complimenting my mother on her nursing skills. Actually, her skills were limited: Vicks vapour rub on the chest, mercury thermometer check each day and nil by mouth except milk of magnesia. If I got out of bed, there was the threat of corporal punishment. Eventually, the threat of bedsores made me feel well enough to go to school. My friends laughed at me for not being able to do anything while I was sick, my mother would say their parents had no discipline.

My wife did not allow me to pass on my mother's methods to our children, though not for want of trying, but the sign of a softer approach to patient care that is now prevalent in our more modern, patient-first NHS.

N Is for **Night Interruptions**

A good night's sleep is crucial but rare in hospital. Sounds that you don't notice in the daytime become exaggerated at night; sounds that are blotted out by other noise in the bustle of daytime noise become the major noise in the dark. Lights out still leaves a glow of light in the corridor that permeates sheets, blankets and eyelids. Shadows and monitor lights play on the ceiling. People around you breathe, snore, talk in their sleep, rustle in their sheets and fart during the night. Fellow patients wander out of the bay, go to the toilet and come back (usually). Sometimes, not in that order. Nurses float in and out performing observations and attending to patient needs. It all creates an aura of noise without noise, the sounds of silence. It is amazing how many people are awake at night, unless I was one of the lucky ones who could sleep OK most of the time. People grunt and groan, watch TV, walk around the corridors and sometimes, seem to be eating as much as they do in the daytime.

N Is for **Nurses**

The nurses are the engine of the NHS. They have multiple functions. I have put together a job spec for nurses from what I have seen them really do.

Be firm: Patients tend to give a lot of excuses as to why they can't do things. Nurses have to see through the charades and tell people what to do. Difficult with miserable old men for sure.

Smile at all times: Nurses approach all tasks with a smile. They are like the clowns on the stage, they act with smiles and witticisms; yet they may go backstage to the unseen areas and have a good cry sometimes.

To laugh at all the jokes and comments they will have heard many times before: Patient humour is fairly standard humour, groups of men certainly like being looked after by a group of ladies, it always brings out the best in their humour.

Be able to clean you: I only had one bed bath in hospital that I can remember. It is a job that nurses carry out with military precision. They will ignore all the private part jokes they have heard before and discard them with the usual smile. I heard one nurse say to a man in the bed next to me, "Goodness, Sir, can you put the mouse back in the house."

Change your bedding: Every day, without fail, you are moved into the chair and they replace your very creased bedding with crisp, fresh, new bedding, locked in place with hospital corners on the sheets. Clean sheet night, every night —one of the hospital luxuries. I would hate to be in charge of the washing machine.

Shave you prior to an operation, nurses seem to relish these opportunities; they have complete control and a mechanical device to work on you with. When I was shaved for my operation, the nurse laughed all the way through her task leaving me as a hairless, plucked turkey next to a mound.

Tie up your gowns: Hospital gowns tie up at the back. A poorly tied gown can give other people a shocking rear image that may set them back weeks. But tying the gown is very difficult, nurses are very good at it though.

Feed you: Not so much on their agenda, unless you are very old and frail.

Sit with you and joke with you: Nurses are brilliant at this.

Stab you with needles: "Small scratch" seems to be the universal forewarning that a needle is going in; sometimes, it is in before they have finished the words.

They make tea for you when you're thirsty, get biscuits for you when you're hungry; some nurses have a stockpile of biscuits and tea and will come around outside regulation meal and tea times and provide tea and a biscuit. They instantly become favourites, all men get better with tea, biscuit and a smile.

O Is for **Other Patients**

When you are in a bay of people, some might be better off than you (let's hope they have been told that there are people worse off than them by their visitors) and some may be worse off (allowing you to feel suitably humbled by your own experience). Usually, you can summarise the situation with some critical observations when you arrive for the first time. Are they sitting up out of bed? Are they in bed and look like they have been for a long time? Have they just walked past you? Do they have tubes and wires all over them? Do they talk to you or at least acknowledge you with the man nod, raise of eyebrows and attempt at a smile?

It is true that a group of strange women will start talking together much more quickly than men. When I use the term strange women, I mean women who are strangers to each other rather than who are strange; although in a cardiac ward of six bays, three with four men each and three with four women each, the wards have their fair share of both from my observation. Men are not naturally sociable in small groups, they prefer bigger crowds for social comfort. However, it has been my experience that men, thrown into a situation they cannot escape from, will be forced to start up conversation straight away, usually related initially to their immediate plight. A hospital situation is, luckily, full of starter question opportunities—which ward are you from? What happened to you? How long do you think you will be here for? Before long and especially for men of a certain era, the Escape from Colditz/Great Escape/life in prison banter begins and there is light-hearted talk of escape plans/digging tunnels/bids for freedom.

No doubt, you will feel that your observational escape/prison humour comments have been heard by the nurses and staff for the first time. But believe me, they are nurses and they will have heard every joke and every proposal before. They have been trained to laugh as if it is the first time they have heard your jokes because that is good for caring. They will laugh and smile because that is what they are trained to do, but what you think is an original joke will be forgotten the minute they walk through the door of your bay and enter the door of the next one to be told the same escape joke as if it is new again.

I met a number of interesting people during my stay. As I was waiting for an operation, I lived a stable life as if the ward was a slightly unconventional bed and breakfast, other people came and went and we shared our lives, papers and sweets and statistics for a few days before they moved on to home, operations, new wards and new lives. Two things became apparent to me. People came in from all sorts of situations, some desperate after a collapse, blackout or heart attack and some in more controlled circumstances. All, however, retained a sense of humour in spite of adversity. The second thing that is apparent is that so many heart problems, including heart attacks, can be recovered from with the right attention and medication. It is a positive sign that I will take from here for the future; heart attacks do not have to be fatal and the NHS are experts at getting you through adversity.

I found it therapeutic to share with my daughter, Emma, the characters I came across. To keep me amused, I named them and gave them stories if they were not interesting enough. It helps pass the time and gives some amusement. Here are a couple of snippets from my WhatsApp diary of the people I met in hospital. None of these names are real.

Hi, Ems, I am in the annex with a 90-year-old milkman, an 84-year-old deaf man, who has lost his dog, and an 80-year-old man, who can't move or talk. The deaf man says that he is not ill, just upset and tells me again and again that he took his dog to the vets, for them to put him right and they put him down. He is very confused and tells the same story to everyone who will listen; the regulars amongst us, including the staff, hear the story each morning and evening. He is very tearful and cries each time he tells the story. He blames the vet.

He has lent me two books, a History of Great Liners and a History of Hatfield Aerodrome. I think I will be tested on these tomorrow amongst the tears.

Hi, Ems, a new man arrived. I shall call him Mr Beetroot, he has a small spindly body with a big purple head on his shoulders. He can't talk but I have deduced that the purple head is the reason he is here. Mr Beetroot's wife came to visit him and my deaf friend told her all about his dog. He cried, she comforted him, Mr Beetroot was forgotten. His head looks like it will explode at any minute.

Hi, Ems, new news. Said goodbye to the lads in the annex and I have been moved to a bay of four in the cardiac ward. The man opposite said hello, I will call him Mr Digestive as he has a big tube of digestive biscuits in front of him. Another man is asleep, he has a diabetic sign above him so I will call him Mr Diabetes. The man next to me is 200 years old, I will call him Mr 200-year-old man. Neither of them seems to have a sad pet story to tell me.

Hi, Ems, spent some time with my new friends this morning, Mr Digestive and Mr Diabetes. Normal family people dealing with heart attacks. The nurses have opened the window and I am worried that Mr 200-year-old man will blow away. Mind you, he has just eaten his bodyweight in dinner.

Hi, Ems, Mr Digestive had a procedure and left today; I think he had just run out of biscuits. New man in, he is a big bloke and very rude to nurses. He has been in hospital a lot in life; for convenience, I will call him Mr Grumpy. Mr Diabetes and Mr 200-year-old man are still with us.

Hi, Ems, Mr Grumpy gone to sleep now. Mr Diabetes and I don't like him. Funny how you can make a gang with someone you've just met.

Hi, Ems, Mr Diabetes went on a trip today for a special scan, treated it as a day out with pack lunch and everything. Mr Grumpy has gone and he has been replaced by Mr

Sergeant Major Moustache, seems quite jolly. Mr 200-year-old man has had his preservation order extended to grade one list.

Hi, Ems, Mr Diabetes and Mr Sergeant Major Moustache have left today. Nice guys! Only me and Mr 200-year-old man left. Maureen, the ward chaplaincy volunteer, paid a visit, I feel blessed now that the Lord knows my predicament. A new man has arrived, he is Polish but I think he is really a Russian, possibly a spy, I shall name him Mr Vladimir Sputum. He says that he has a heart problem, but I think he is controlling the Russian mafia on his phone from his bed.

Hi, Ems, Mr Sputum is on a call with his superiors in Moscow, I will have to sleep with one eye open tonight. No sign of poison tipped umbrellas or aerosols except I had an unfortunate glimpse of Mr Sergeant Major Moustache's aerosol when he put his gown on earlier. Mr 200-year-old man had physio today but then had to be embalmed with oxygen.

Hi Ems, Mr Sputum, slung on his little backpack, said goodbye and walked out after being discharged but without his medication; he must have been called out on a mission. Mr Sergeant Major Moustache also discharged so just me and Mr 200-year-old man left. Mr 200-year-old man being filled with preservative gas, so he is looking his best for a family visit tomorrow.

Hi, Ems, two new people today, Mr Moanhamed, who seems to moan a lot but no one can understand him. He is deaf and does not speak much English. At least he does not think it an insult when English people use the commonly taught technique of euro-understanding and shout at him to make him understand them, he thinks it is because he is deaf. I think he has brought his whole family in disguised as pieces of fruit. Then there is a normal person I have talked to, who is interesting and funny, therefore, I shall just call him Brian.

Hi, Ems, Mrs Moanhamed came in tonight with a massive Mother's Day cake, which she proceeded slice up and gave to all of us. Very nice of her and Mr Moanhamed! I shall now call him Mr Mohappymed. Mr Mohappymed goes on long walks with his coat over his pyjamas. I have timed the walks at 35 minutes, I may have to follow him and see where he goes. I think that he may be smoking (Mr Mohappymed was eventually caught outside smoking by his consultant, who gave him a dressing down in the bay. He now puts his coat on after he thinks the consultant has gone home).

Hi, Ems, Mr Mohappymed is now definitely Mr Mo-not-very-happy-med as he fell into the classic trap of over optimism. He was told that he was going home tomorrow on Monday, but it is now Saturday and he has been told again that he can go home tomorrow. For him, the old saying is true—tomorrow never comes. I think this is punishment for his smoking. Brian and I reminiscing about old Harpenden. Brian's old Harpenden is older than mine, he is 20 years older than me.

Hi, Ems, Mr 200-year-old man, unfortunately, passed away last night and a new man from Lithuania has arrived. He is called Ivan, I will call him Mr Ivan the terrible. He claims that he is from Lithuania and his phone and memory have been embedded with a whole back story family pack of pictures and children and grandchildren. He is very keen to show me all the pictures and embed his family in my mind, definitely a KGB training trick. He must be a KGB operative with a new identity. He has been issued with shuffle slippers to make him look like a cardiac patient and look less like a stealth killer. I will have to watch his movements closely. He keeps looking out of the window and then down at his phone. I think he may be getting signals from a handler stationed in acute geriatric. He will be off on a mission later.

Hi, Ems, Mr Ivan has been wheeled off, they say to another ward but I did not recognise the porters. They were dressed in black. Probably taking him off to a blacked-out van in the underground car park. Mission underway, I think.

This section is dedicated to the friends I made in my confinement (no real names provided), Derek and Charlie. The 90-year-old milkman, Mr Stroke, Mr Diabetes, Mr Digestive, Mr 200-Year-Old Man, Mr Beetroot, Captain Birdseye, Mr Grumpy, Sergeant Major Moustache, Mr Paul

Price, Mr Young Hugh Bonneville, Mr Vladimir Sputum, Mr Moanhamed (who became Mr Mohappymed), Mr Brian, Mr Ivan the terrible, Magneto, Del Boy, Mr Polish Peter, Mr Walter White, Mr Liverpool and Mr Wobble.

P Is for **the Pharmacist**

The pharmacist is the last barrier that divides the laws and rules of the institution and the freedom of home. The discharge nurse gives you the papers—a pass out—neighbours or family relatives come in to take you home (unless you have been forgotten or forcefully erased), parties are booked to welcome you home and car parking is carefully timed to get you out in less than the one hour before the charges rocket up.

However, as I have seen in my observations, this is another case of misplaced optimism. Always allow at least 24 hours to get medication up from the bowels of the pharmacy. For whatever the reason, and of course, pharmacy get the blame but it might not be them, the cogs of this final releasing machine work extremely slowly.

The misplaced optimism at this stage of a stay is crushing. I have listened in on the phone calls as more than one human being has slid down the ladder of optimism from "I'll be home before lunchtime" to "I'll be home before it gets dark" to "Save me some welcome home party cake" to "I may be in here another night". As the pharmacist gets the blame, there is not a uniform that I see a lot on the wards, and I don't think it is widely advertised on the "know your staff" chart for fear of reprisals; bags of tablets are delivered like takeaway lunches by mysterious runners, who run off and disappear into the fabric of the hospital.

P Is for **Phlebotomist**

The phlebotomist are unusually jolly people, who come in pushing their white trolley in front of them like a defensive screen. They love to come in all smiles and then ask the question, "Can I take some blood from you?" Usually followed by a calming term of endearment, such as "darling" or "sweetheart". They are going to take the blood, come what may, but asking permission first makes you think that you have asked for this bloodthirsty service. No one ever says, "No, you can't." They are probably the most feared hospital operator and they know it, as they have only one purpose in the hospital. They have a special trolley with wheels that make their own squeaky sound so patients know this is not the tea trolley coming. Being the subject of the routines of various comedians over the years and vampire jokes aside, the phlebotomists are very efficient and friendly, but they don't come out much in the daytime or eat too much garlic. What do phlebotomists talk about after work? Do they meet together in darkened rooms or mix with normal people? Do their partners sleep with the light on?

Phlebotomists will always round off their visit by shouting, "See you later!"

I don't know why I answered, "Yep, see you later," because they are the one person you don't want to see again, but they have cleverly lulled you into a false sense of security again. The institution strikes again.

I have had two phlebotomists on the bay at the same time, circling around. What is the term for more than one phlebotomist, are they phlebotomi? One phlebotomist said that a group of phlebotomists are called "a bloody nuisance".

Phlebotomy humour! Phlebotomists group together in the bowels of the hospital but quickly scatter when approached.

P Is for **Porters**

Porters are the silent cogs that move everything round in the hospital, transporting patients around in beds and wheelchairs to their various scans and procedures. They are very protective of their chairs and all seem to have special secret cupboards full of mobility equipment. The wheelchairs may look normal but all have been adapted from standard machines like the robots in Robot Wars. Special door opening fixtures added, cornering aids and anti-flip devices are added. Many of the porters are volunteers. There is probably classis men in sheds type space under the hospital, where they gather in the semi-dark and fix their equipment, soup it up and pimp their machines and laugh about the crazy times. They are all on laughing gas and all enjoy giving patients the nearest experience to a roller coaster that many will ever experience. You are used as a battering ram door opener, you are skidded round corners on two wheels and all without a belt on. They share hilarious but completely untrue (I think) stories of people losing feet and arms on trips around. What a great job they do!

R Is for **Rating Your Stay**

A guilty pleasure of mine is the Channel Four series, Four in a Bed, where couples that run bed and breakfasts visit each other's bed and breakfasts and then rate them; firstly, on a form of simple questions and secondly, by paying what they think the room is worth. There is always some animosity when couples do not pay the full price or mark down the opponent's B and B and then have to defend their decisions, while other couples shout gamesmanship.

Can you rate a stay in hospital? How do you rate a stay? It is not a place you come to stay in by choice or a place you want to stay in for long. However, you often end up staying in a ward for longer than your longest summer holiday hotel. All experiences have some positive points and, no doubt, some negative points.

I think the six questions on the "Four in a Bed" form should be applicable to your stay in hospital. I have listed the categories here and added some comments from my stay.

How were your hosts in the ward?

Comments: Over attentive at times, kept waking me up to see how I was every four hours. Came in and made bed at 06.00 in the morning.

How clean was the ward?

Comments: Overzealous with cleaning. Floors swept and mopped every morning at 07.00. Anti-bacterial hand cleanser everywhere, wouldn't have expected this in a B and B.

How were the facilities on the ward?

Comments: No en suite, just a sink and taps. Shared toilets further up the corridor. I was not expecting to spend my stay with three other men. No Amazon Echo to turn the lights out.

No tea and coffee making facilities, Wi-Fi or full Sky TV. TV only available for four hours.

How did you sleep on the ward?

Comments: Couldn't open windows. Pillows flat. Bed able to move into a variety of positions. No duvets but extra blankets available. Room is very warm, windows don't open very far.

How were the meals on the ward?

Comments: Small portions, a basic menu, breakfasts restricted to porridge, serials and toast. No full English breakfasts available. No eggs benedict and no eggs Florentine. Actually, no eggs.

Would you stay on the ward again?

Comments: No, not if I can help it.

The ward had adopted a different approach to rating your stay. Through the heading of "Introducing Your Friends and Family", they ask the question:

We would like to know how likely are you to recommend this ward to your friends and family if they needed similar care or treatment.

This is part of a ward survey you fill in on discharge, rating each category.

There are three categories of answers: extremely likely (a positive score), likely (a neutral score) and neither likely or unlikely, unlikely or extremely unlikely (a negative score). Unlike Four in a Bed, this is not a competition, you will not have to sit in front of your nurses at the end of your stay and explain any negative scores while they shout "gamesmanship!" However, you may be asked to explain your selection from the nine different categories that come under the heading "Which gender would you like to be known as?"

As I see it, there are some issues with this method of rating a ward. One, in an emergency heart-related situation, cardiac ward is likely to be the place you are sent whether you rated it likely or unlikely in a previous visit. Or if you have been before, do they present you with your previous survey and offer you the opportunity to go somewhere else? Your argument that you might want to go somewhere else because you rated the breakfast on the third morning poor because the toast was colder than usual will not wash when your health is at stake. Secondly, when would you want to recommend any hospital stay to family or relatives? I would have to tick the unlikely box at that point. It's not like recommending a restaurant, which you can recommend to a friend and get a free voucher for a meal for two.

S Is for **Statistics**

Statistics drive you each day—these are the numbers that visitors want to know, your ward colleagues will laugh at, nurses need to know and you become strangely addicted to knowing and recording. Blood pressure, heartbeat, oxygen level and weight are the most common daily stats, and they form a set of numbers that you can use to compete with your colleagues in a variety of competitions. You can also discuss them behind their backs when they are in the shower or having a scan. There are ample opportunities to gather statistics, from the four hourly observation visits to the daily or every other day blood tests. With the internet availability, patients can look up what range they should be in, as we often look up BMI weight charts but different consultants look at different things. I wish they would abandon BMI usage as being short, it makes me constantly obese unless my waist measurement comes down to 30cm.

S Is for **Small Rooms**

When you are taken away for scans and tests, you often go down into the bowels of the hospital, into small rooms that people seem to inhabit and never leave to go up to the daylight. For me, one such room was the office of the man who carried out the breathing /lung function tests, who lived in the most out of the way secret place. His room was small, badly lit and full of technical machines including a booth that looked like a shower cubicle with a seat and a tumble drier hose in it. I joked that it looked like a time machine and he looked at me as if I had rumbled his lifetime's secret work. He insisted in collecting and delivering his own patients, rather than employ porters and whistled constantly as he drove me around as if to disorientate me and make me forget the route. All his machines had tubes and nozzles and he had a radio on the windowsill that played hippy sounding music, while he connected me up. The window was small and looked out onto a wall, an aspect that suitably disguised his top-secret activities. I was convinced that one day, he would emerge from his little room 30 years younger than when he went in, or Elvis would emerge and just walk off down the corridor. This was just one of many small rooms and, no doubt, one of many secret projects that were going on in the hospital without anyone knowing, any one of which, if it came to fruition would fund the NHS for a lifetime.

S Is for **Shuffling**

What makes you want to shuffle in hospital? Not only shuffle around the ward and corridors but shuffle belongings into new piles and new places. My wife bought me my first ever slippers while I was in hospital. I think they were marketed as special hospital slippers. They forced me to slow down and shuffle my feet across the floor because if I lifted the slipper, it would fall off my foot. Only the clawing action of my toes kept them on. Shuffling identifies you as a patient and not a visitor; any escape attempt can be foiled before you can get speed up and if you do make it off the ward, you are likely to break your neck on the stairs.

But shuffling belongings into piles, why do we fall into that trap? Is it a relief from the boredom? I've seen old people and dementia patients shuffle through piles of things, but I have never done such a thing before myself. And yet I find myself doing this past time regularly, create some space on the table, fill some space on the table, check pants and socks in the cupboard, recheck pants and socks. It fills the time between meals. It is nice to have a lot of stuff because it can all be re-arranged regularly; minimalist people must get very bored in hospital with so little to arrange.

T Is for **Trolleys**

It may seem super nerdy to include something as mundane as trolleys in this run through the NHS, but when you hear things before you see them appear through the doors, it is important to distinguish between trolleys of hope and trolleys of doom. Hope trolleys are meal trolleys, tea trolleys and water trolleys. These trolleys are pushed by smiley kitchen staff, whose uniforms and demeanour exude helpfulness and hope. Trolleys of doom are phlebotomist's trolleys, observations trolleys and drugs trolleys. These trolleys provide no added value to the day and remind you that you are ill. They are all pushed by nurses and sisters, which adds to the feeling of doom. The wheels of each trolley have a unique sound, maybe a sticking wheel, a creaky suspension, too much weight. If the NHS ever decided to oil the trolley wheels regularly, this guessing game would be over and the trolleys would last much longer.

U Is for **Uniform**

Two facts of life: one, human beings come in all shapes and sizes; two, hospital nursing uniforms do not. I applaud the NHS for its uniform policy, the ranks and the roles of the various people involved in the NHS becomes apparent very quickly from the wall chart showing distinctive tunics and epaulettes—a bit like a guide to the Royal Navy. You quickly associate some uniforms with safe people of no threat such as cleaners, volunteers, meal providers, discharge nurses, porters and students; basically anyone you can have a laugh with or who provide food and tea. Then, there are those uniforms with more sinister roles like sisters, matrons and phlebotomists; basically people who can hurt you or make decisions that can hurt you. Nurses' uniforms I think come in one or maybe two sizes and lengths. This leads to a blurring of the meaning of uniformity, maybe unfairly described as a variety of round pegs in square holes. The perfectly creased, starched uniforms of the old regime with belts and hats and regulation shoes inspected by the matron each morning have given way to a looser approach, let us say a more individual approach to what is smart. The average employee fits the uniform very well, nurses look very smart in their dresses and tunics, smart trousers or tights, demonstrating discipline to the cause by wearing regulation fob watches, smart belts and hair in regulation tidiness. Unfortunately, average is exactly what it says, it is the middle of a large sample. Even more unfortunately, for the NHS, the sample from which "average" is taken comes from a mix of eastern European countries once populated by the Norsemen of Scandinavia, the result of which is very tall thin people, and the Pacific rim countries populated on the whole by petite slim people. The world is full of less than or greater than average people (or as we have to say in 2018, the world is full of more diverse people releasing their inner character), who demonstrate the limitations, or again in a more optimistic world, challenges presented by nursing uniform size guides.

Disclaimer: Please note that in the above observation, I made reference to roles and nurses; at no point did I suggest any difference between males, females and other non-gender, specific/gender fluid individuals.

Patients also have uniforms. Gowns and pyjamas in a fresh floral print was the design chosen at my hospital. It gave even the most ill patients a healthy look. However, it can give the impression that you have walked into one of the old-style lunatic asylums, especially when the uniform is paired with the shuffle slippers. Patient uniforms can, however, make you extremely popular amongst people in the hospital. When you are wheeled around the hospital for various scans and procedures, sat on a trolley, your bed or on a chair, in your uniform and with a hospital blanket around you, everyone looks at you and smiles. If you can add a pathetic smile as well, men feel obliged to say hello and women look at you with a mothering look. It gives you the feeling that there will always be someone who would take you in if your family forgot to or decided not to claim you after discharge. There is probably a special lost patient department in the hospital somewhere, where sympathetic hospital visitors can go and claim an unwanted patient—a bit like Battersea Dogs Home. One day, Paul O Grady will make a programme about it.

W Is for **Waiting**

Patients spend their lives waiting—waiting for procedures, waiting for medication, waiting for doctors to make decisions, waiting for meals, waiting for results, waiting for discharge nurses, waiting for transfers, waiting for scans, waiting for the smell of a sneaky fart to disperse, waiting for beds, waiting to use the toilet. In fact, nothing is gained in hospital without waiting. With the need for waiting comes the need for patience. Every patient has their patience threshold—the limit that once crossed sends even the calmest people into a raging frenzy. I decided to commission a study by myself of the patient's patience threshold limit, very little has been written about this phenomenon before. I will share it with you, the reader. In line with the stool chart and the Pain Threshold Chart and Borg Exertion Chart, I have put the 10 types of patient patience into a chart. I had the opportunity to observe 26 people pass through cardiac care, a department not known for speed and I, therefore, had a good sample size to work from. I could rate them on their patient's patience threshold and also observe how patient's patience starts to break down in the face of constant waiting. 1-3 is OK, 4-6 requires loving care management, 7-8 needs comfort and attention and 9-10 need physical restraint.

The Pointless Patient's Patience Chart of Patient Practice

1 Very patient: Usually new people, disorientated, not understanding what is going on. This period lasts different lengths of time depending on the person, it may last a day or weeks. If this stage lasts weeks, then it is unlikely that the patient will ever get to stage six or higher. He is a very patient patient, he has been waiting patiently for England to win the World Cup again since 1966.

2 Still patient: Been in a while but still optimistic of an early exit, the outside world is still within grasping distance. Promises can still be believed. He is a slow burner.

3 Patient: Signs of realisation taking over from optimism. Optimism becomes hope but hope springs eternal; he may get suddenly depressed and start using the word please in a begging way. He is easily pacified with some more false promises. Beware, he will move on to stage five or six quite quickly.

4 Patient with concerns: Doctor's promises start to become difficult to believe. Can be pacified but with more complicated stories and can be anesthetised with medical jargon.

5 Odd signs of impatience: Fidgeting, leg and finger tapping, sleeping a lot in the daytime, commenting on the time and date, these are signs of the impatience growing. At this stage, it comes and goes, the body language says I don't know why I am here and I don't know what is going on. If it lasts a day, he will get to stage seven or eight very quickly, maybe within one day.

6 Constant signs of impatience: The above signs become constant, nurses get asked what is going on, the only question for doctors is when can I go home. He knows exactly to the hour how long he has been in hospital and wants everyone to know it. All optimism gone.

7 Impatient: Hints of aggression, muttering, shrugging of shoulders, swearing under breath, asking for doctors all the time interspersed with taking to bed and sleeping a lot. Starts to demand answers and dates.

8 Very impatient: Very argumentative, disagrees with the nurses and doctors, threatens to go home but at this stage, he won't.

9 No patience at all: Characterised by agitated walking around, talking to himself, arguments turn to shouting matches. Suddenly, no food is good enough. Probably an arsenal fan where frustration comes on quite quickly.

10 Patience broken: Agitation, uses verbal abuse, flaying arms, pulls out drains and catheters and leaves without discharge or medication. Re-admitted 10 days later.

I am still waiting for a reply from the NHS about my work. But I am a patient with type 1 patience.

W Is for **the Ward**

The ward is where you spend most of the time. It becomes your home, your bedroom and all this shared with, in my case, three other men. As it is home, it also needs to become your source of entertainment, a source of comradery and laughter.

Of course, 50 years ago, the ward was a different place. It was managed by the matron and wards were long corridors with lines of beds either side and a nurse sat in the middle. Now, wards are divided into bays of four people; each bay has its own rotating staff and they don't stand over you all day. Thus, there is ample time for conversation with the other colleagues in your bay.

The ward is a living being with its own sounds, smells and sights. It also looks the same every day and every day becomes the same. Weekends are slightly quieter without doctors moving around but the rest of the routine is the same.

As each day is the same regardless of weekends or weekdays, the ward has a special clock that displays the time, the date and the day of the week. It is important to display the day as each day blurs into the next so it is nice to know when weekends are. Wards are fitted with special clocks that go slower than ordinary clocks so that the average day in hospital is two or three hours longer than the days on the outside. When you come out of hospital, the inside time and the outside time realign themselves. It makes looking at watches irrelevant and phones only useful for communicating, not telling the time.

Each bed has a table and a cupboard for possessions. Tables are the cantilever type that will pull over the bed and are just awkwardly the wrong size to make them useful for anything except standing the glass and water jug and standard size satsuma. Standing things on the tables is a balancing act, many times drinks bottles, plastic cups and satsumas fall to the floor. The floors are cleaned after a fashion every day, but for my own safety, I reduced the five-second pick up rule for food to three seconds to avoid risk of infection. Cupboards are all different but have just not enough space to put anything in easily. It took my wife three days of re-arranging to get my whole home life in my cupboard. Determination and secret visits to the charity shop paid off eventually.

The ward beeps as if it has a heartbeat, the background sound of monitor jingles. There is a special hospital silence, never really silent but constantly humming in the background. You get used to thinking that this is silence; when you get out and experience real silence again, it is difficult to embrace it. I can imagine now how hard it was for soldiers returning from war to integrate back into a normal society, yearning to go back into a regimented world with its defined days. Above this background silence, there is the beep of the heartbeat monitors, the heavy breathing of boredom and sleep, and the occasional tipping out of water followed by cursing as the water spills over the edge of the cup and runs along the sloping tabletop to the floor.

The ward is a flexible being, different patients come and go and different nurses each day depending on the rota (offering the temptation to make the escape jokes as if they are new) but essentially, the view remains the same and the routine remains the same—other beds, other patients, other tables.

Each day on the ward is the same. Routine is important in an institution and believe me, you very quickly become institutionalised. Each day starts with observations at 06.00. Always good to make a mental note of the numbers for blood pressure, temperature and pulse as you can use this for discussion later on. Then you need to orientate yourself with which day it is and the date. Once the nurses have established that there is life, the lights go on, the blinds are pulled back, and you can see the world outside that you are not allowed to access. Normal people walking around, driving to work, going to appointments, going shopping, looking forward to the weekend knowing it will be different from the week—a snapshot of reality.

After observations, it is bed-making time followed by breakfast and the obligatory issue of medicine and pills. Every night in hospital is clean sheet night; that feeling of clean crisp linen is some compensation for being here. In one bed making session, the nurses unfolded my new sheets to find knots in them. Could those sheets tell a tale of escape or attempted escape? Were they found dangling from a first-floor window, a pair of slippers lying on the ground nearby?

While breakfast is being consumed, the jolly cleaner comes around; her job is to sweep away the last remnants of hope from the new optimists and mop up any last optimism of an early exit, all with a smile on her face and a cheery conversation. I became convinced when I left that despair smelt like flash floor cleaner. The bay is cleaned, bins emptied, floors swept and washed and then all of a sudden, all goes quiet. There is a pause while people get over the disappointment of finishing breakfast, start to look forward to dinner, wash and shower and shuffle the piles of things on tables and beds into new piles ready to be reshuffled later.

Like flash, there will be some smells that will never leave you after hospital life. Everywhere has a hospital smell, the smell of the fresh linen, the smell of your meals and the occasional smell of the outside, such as when the visitors opposite sneak in a McDonald's.

Then there is a sudden surge of activity—ward doctors, phlebotomists—the ward comes alive with questions, hand gestures and the issuing of standard doses of hope and optimism.

After 9.00, ward life becomes a time of waiting, sleeping, reading, going off ward for procedures, doctor's visits and checks. There are three and a half hours to kill before dinner. Hope and optimism wear off. A procedure or trip off the ward is a welcome break to kill vital time; otherwise, time is spent sleeping and reading, walking up and down if you can, drinking water, more shuffling and doing puzzle books.

Cleaners come and go, ladies asking for dinner and supper orders, nurses dish out pills. Dinner appears and all too quickly, it is over. A glance at the clock shows five hours until supper. But these five hours is the part of the day when the visitors can come, a welcome break during the afternoon; welcome as it is a time of variety, each visitor has a different story to tell, different news to impart, as well as wanting to know the hospital latest. They are welcome as long as their presence does not interfere with supper. Supper duly comes and after supper, the visitors drift off, and it is time for a change into leisure wear ready for final pills, checks, maybe a chat with your ward mates and then lights out at 22.00.

Each patient has a magnetic board on the wall above their bed. It has your location number, in my case D1, and sections for when you achieve your badges. Badges are triangular or rectangular magnetic plaques that indicate your status. I only ever achieved my nil by mouth badge, but other people had multiple badges like special diets, diabetic, nil by mouth, danger-falls, gluten free and risk of falls. In the scouts, these people would have been the goody, goody scouts with an armful of badges.

No one wanted the butterfly badge—dementia.

An inmate should be able to earn badges, in the same tradition as the scouts, when in hospital for any length of time. It would be a way of educating oneself whilst being in hospital, helping the nurses and filling the overhead magnetic board. As with the scouts, there would be three levels of achievement: core badges, activity badges and challenge badges. Core badges would be bed making, advanced bed making, arse wiping, bed bath, nursing care, making tea and issuing and collecting meals. Activity badges would be taking blood, inserting a cannula, connecting an IV drip. Challenge badges would be MRI scanner operator, general nursing, house officer and cardiac consultant. Develop the NHS from within.

I think it is an NHS plan for patients to be provided with sleep deprivation, so that they spend more time asleep during the day and thus, give less hassle. At night time, lights go on and off, nurses come in and out, people snore and fart and grunt and cough, patients go to the toilet. Pillows deflate and have to be re arranged. After a few days, all you want to do is sleep during the day, especially in the morning when there is time to kill. Your mind plays tricks, you dream weird dreams, imagine your old life. One Flew Over the Cuckoo's Nest. As you drift in and out of consciousness, you can identify the footsteps of those around you—the urgent, purposeful footsteps of the nurses and staff, the faltering interrupted steps of the first-time visitor, the apologetic footsteps of the ward volunteers and the shuffling, resigned steps of patients. Only the feet of the ward chaplaincy volunteer make no noise, as they angelically sneak up on you as you doze.

W Is for **Ward Chaplaincy Volunteer**

I am not religious but I understand the vital work that these people do in generally caring for a lot of people in hospital who are lonely or worried. They do offer a great assistance and can be abused for the privilege, so bearing in mind that they are volunteers, I have nothing but praise for them. The only comment I would make is that they should be uniformed like all other staff so that stable people, like myself, can see them coming and join the ranks of people pretending to be asleep when they appear in the bay. Only one chaplaincy volunteer came in with a uniform, the Salvation Army volunteer, but she had secretly crafted her uniform to look very similar to the hospital student's uniform. A quick glance left you off guard, even after the slight confusion of seeing a 70-year-old in a student's nurse uniform did not. Here lies the benefit of experience, of being an inmate for a while and being one who has already completed the Dorling Kindersley I Spy book of hospital ward life, which includes ward visitor recognition charts.

W Is for **Ward Volunteers**

The ward chaplaincy volunteer has a purpose—to bring love and compassion to those that believe. Ward volunteers have a purpose that I am not sure of. They are kindly older ladies with a green tabard and clear plastic apron, who mean well and smile a lot but achieve very little except causing chaos ahead of and behind the kitchen staff who are trying to stick to their well-drilled plan of serving food and recovering plates. Ward volunteers walk into and out of each bay collecting the odd tray and cup, giving out the odd dessert and making compliments about how well people have eaten in the same way as a nan would encourage a four-year-old child. The ward kitchen staff do not pamper to such requests or give compliments to anyone. They carry out a job of high efficiency, precision feeding and clearing up.

W Is for **the Weekend**

Hoorah, it's the weekend! But in hospital, apart from the special clock with the day written on it that tells you it is the weekend, inmates in hospital would never know. Each day is the same. Or is it....? Having spent a few weekends in the wards, I am becoming more convinced that there is something more sinister afoot. I believe a gentle nerve gas is wafted through the bays at weekends making everyone much sleepier than usual. You wake up now and again for meals and blood tests and then you are allowed to sleep again, while the nurses have a party and a rest. I have proven my concept by crafting a crude gas mask from a towel that I managed to smuggle back into the bay one Friday and then forcing myself awake early on Saturday morning. By urinating on the towel (a trick I learnt from reading about gas attacks in the First World War), I could prevent the onset of sleepiness when the gas was released. One word of warning: be careful while urinating on a towel in the morning when you are on anti-water retention tablets. And so, after the usual guard checks had been completed and my bay colleagues had fallen asleep and the nurses had given up looking for the source of the urine smell, I could go for a walk and see what was going on in this silent Saturday world. As I suspected, the nurses were all huddled around their nurse station and all the other patients were asleep. I knew that I wouldn't be free for long without being discovered but that was part of the experiment, would they try and bundle me back into bed before I could escape, proving they had something to hide? Of course, the reason they came after me so quickly could have been the yellow stain on the front of my shirt or the dripping towel wrapped around my head or the smell of piss.

But Seriously

When I look back on my stay in hospital, I am glad I took time to record the goings on, and as it happened, the people I met made my stay in hospital a positive experience. But for many, especially those going into hospital, it can be a daunting experience. It can also be a sudden unexpected experience and mean the upsetting of plans and dreams. From my experiences, I have put together a top ten list of ideas that may help you battle the effects of the institution.

1. Talk to other people, you may only know them for a brief time or you may become lifelong friends, but talking to people is a great tonic and illness breaks down all barriers of class and creed.
2. Walk as much as possible, push yourself to walk whenever you can, it makes a change of scene; you may meet more people and it is good for general health.
3. Laugh with your fellow patients, laughter is the greatest medicine, although it can hurt as well.
4. Eat well, fuel for the engine as my son calls it, not eating is not good for health.
5. Stay regular, which means walking, eating fruit and drinking juices.
6. Take a good book or some other distraction for when things are quiet.
7. If you physically can get up and dressed each day, do not sit in pyjamas all day, every day. It will make you feel better and more human.
8. Be patient. Frustration and anger, I saw a lot in hospital. When you go in to the institution, you will

face delays, cancellations, lots of waiting and vague promises. Be prepared for this and it will not wind you up so much.

9. Always welcome visitors.

10. Obey the nurses' instructions, they are there to advise you on how to get better and to assist you with that task. Moaning, shouting and arguing with nurses does not help with recovery.

Epilogue

My mum died on 3 April 2018 after a short illness ended up with her being in the hospital where I was. I, unfortunately, had moved on to another hospital when she died. She had fought her last battle with dignity, Savlon and milk of magnesia, and complete disregard for hospital advice on modern methods. When she died, I was on the eve of my operation so the family hid the fact that she had died until they knew that I was coming out and they knew that my operation had been successful. Absolutely the right thing to do. As I sat at my bed with my laptop trying to come up with the Epilogue, a suitable homage to all those I met, I was told the news of her passing and so, the first line of this part of my book came easy. I had already in filled her into my earlier stories and this story completes my homage to her.

The NHS couldn't save my mum in the end, although they tried mightily hard on many occasions. Was it the stubborn wartime spirit? But she wasn't prepared to help herself in the end and at 91, a bit of listening on her part would have helped. The NHS helps millions of people every day at Harefield Heart Hospital, where I was for some time; the staff perform miracles bringing people back from the brink. And it all happens in the quirky atmosphere that we call the hospital, which I have tried to describe here.